LEONARDO & HIS TIMES
 LIFE
 LIGHT
 MAMMAL
 MANET
 MARS

 MEDICINE
 MEDIEVAL LIFE
 MONET
 MONEY
 MUMMY
 MUSIC
 MYTHOLOGY
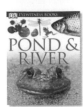 NASCAR

 NORTH AMERICAN INDIAN
 OCEAN
 OLYMPICS
 PERSPECTIVE
 PHOTOGRAPHY
 PIRATE
 PLANT
 POND & RIVER

 PREHISTORIC LIFE
 PRESIDENTS
 PYRAMID
 RELIGION
 RENAISSANCE
 REPTILE
 RESCUE
 ROBOT

 ROCKS & MINERALS
 RUSSIA
 SEASHORE
 SHAKESPEARE
 SHARK
 SHELL
 SHIPWRECK
 SKELETON

 SOCCER
 SPACE EXPLORATION
 SPORTS
 SPY
 SUBMARINE
 SUPER BOWL
 TECHNOLOGY
 TEXAS

 TIME & SPACE
 TITANIC
 TRAIN
 VIETNAM WAR
 VIKING

 VOLCANO & EARTHQUAKE
 WATERCOLOR
 WORLD SERIES
 WORLD WAR I

Louisburg Library District No. 1

206 S. Broadway

P.O. Box 398

Louisburg, KS 66053

913-837-2217

 WORLD WAR II

DEMCO

Eyewitness
ECOLOGY

Apparatus to measure
water quality

Red seaweed

Squid

Starfish

Population of woodlice

Merlin

Tullgren
funnel

Eyewitness
ECOLOGY

Written by
STEVE POLLOCK

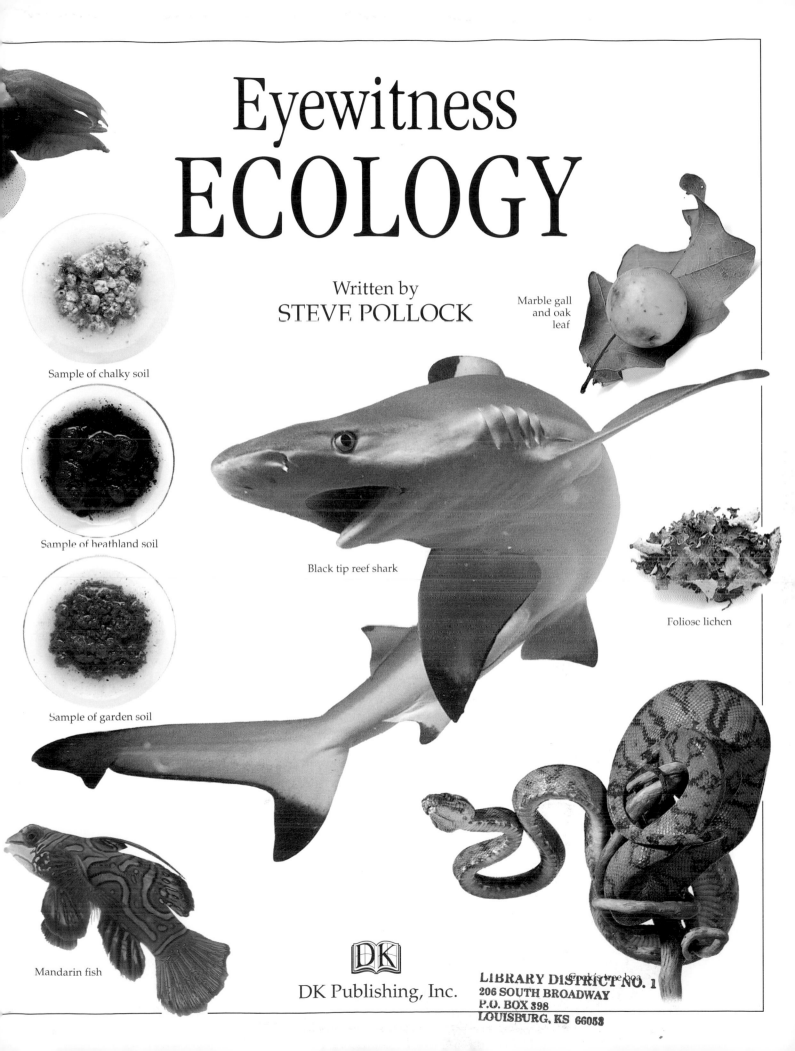

Sample of chalky soil

Sample of heathland soil

Sample of garden soil

Marble gall and oak leaf

Black tip reef shark

Foliose lichen

Mandarin fish

DK Publishing, Inc.

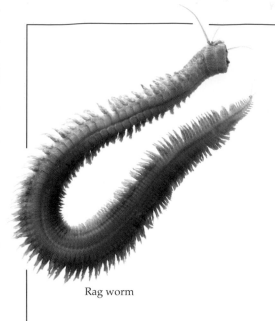

Garfish

Pine cones

LONDON, NEW YORK, MUNICH,
MELBOURNE, and DELHI

Project Editor Ian Whitelaw
Art Editor Val Cunliffe
Designer Helen Diplock
Production Louise Daly
Picture Research Catherine O'Rourke
Managing Editor Josephine Buchanan
Managing Art Editor Lynne Brown
Special Photography Frank Greenaway,
The Natural History Museum, London
Editorial Consultant Dr David Harper,
University of Sussex
U.S. Editor Charles A. Wills
U.S. Consultant Professor O. Roger Anderson,
Teachers College, Columbia University

REVISED EDITION
Editors Barbara Berger, Laura Buller
Editorial assistant John Searcy
Publishing director Beth Sutinis
Senior designer Tai Blanche
Designers Jessica Lasher,
Diana Catherines
Photo research Chrissy McIntyre
Art director Dirk Kaufman
DTP designer Milos Orlovic
Production Ivor Parker

Pine seeds

Horse
chestnut seed

Sweet
chestnut
seed

This edition published in the United States in 2005
by DK Publishing, Inc.
375 Hudson Street, New York, NY 10014

05 06 07 08 09 10 9 8 7 6 5 4 3 2 1

A catalog record for this book is
available from the Library of Congress.

ISBN 0-7566-1387-6 (HC) 0-7566-1396-5 (ALB)

Color reproduction by Colourscan, Singapore
Printed in China by Toppan Printing Co.,
(Shenzhen) Ltd.

Discover more at
www.dk.com

Rag worm

Yeast culture in petri dish

Wolf spider

Orkney vole

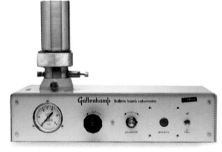

Cuckoo wrasse

Bomb calorimeter

Field digger wasp
capturing fly

Contents

Plants, fungi, and seeds of
the deciduous forest floor

What is ecology?

No living thing or group of living things exists in isolation. All organisms, both plants and animals, need energy and materials from the environment in order to survive, and the lives of all kinds of living things, or species, affect the lives of others. Ecology is the study of the relationships between living things (within species and between different species) and between them and their environment. Humans have always studied living things in their natural environment in order to hunt and to gather food, but as a scientific discipline ecology is relatively new. Ecologists do study species in their natural context ("in the field"), but they also carry out laboratory studies and experiments. Fieldwork involves the collection of information to see what happens to particular species – such as population numbers, diet, form, size, and behavior. Ecologists also study physical aspects of the environment – such as the composition of rocks, soil, air, and water. The data can be used to identify patterns and trends, and some of these can be tested in the laboratory.

PROVIDING THE ESSENTIALS
All organisms depend on a variety of factors in the environment. These include light, temperature, the chemicals or nutrients that enable plants and animals to grow and, most important, water. In an artificial context, like a garden, all these factors must be provided if the plants are to grow successfully.

STICKING TOGETHER
Individual animals very rarely live on their own. They are usually to be found in a population, interacting with others of their species, as these woodlice are doing. Members of a population compete with each other for resources, including food and shelter. They also interbreed to produce new generations, ensuring the continued life of the population as it copes with seasonal and long-term changes in the environment. Studies of particular populations are common in ecology.

BACKYARD ECOLOGY
A garden provides a small-scale model of life all over planet Earth. Rocks and soil, rain and wind, animals and plants exist together, each affecting the others directly and indirectly, gradually changing the landscape. A plant takes up chemicals from the soil, flowers, and produces seeds. A mouse eats the seeds, and a cat preys on the mouse. The plant dies and begins to decay. A worm eats the rotting plant and returns the chemicals to the soil. Ecology is the study of these kinds of interaction among plants, animals, and the nonliving elements in the environment.

Algae on pot

Heather

Flowering plant

Cat (predator)

Lichen-covered rock

Soil provides essential nutrients for plant growth

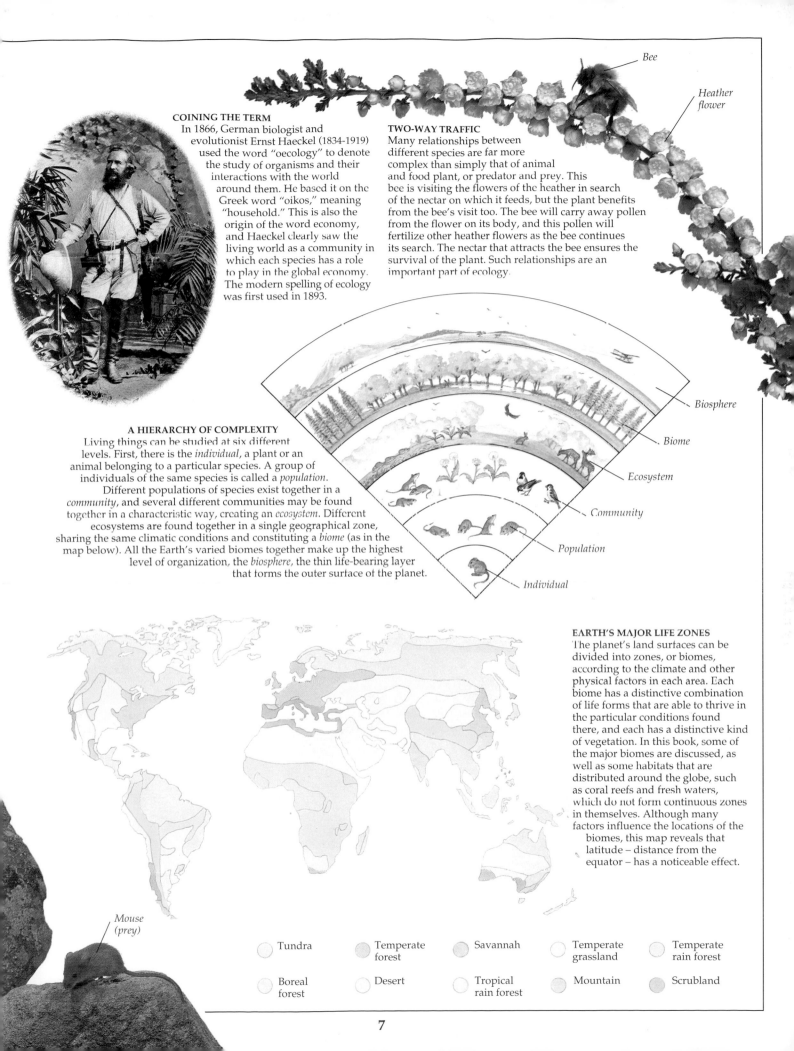

COINING THE TERM
In 1866, German biologist and evolutionist Ernst Haeckel (1834-1919) used the word "oecology" to denote the study of organisms and their interactions with the world around them. He based it on the Greek word "oikos," meaning "household." This is also the origin of the word economy, and Haeckel clearly saw the living world as a community in which each species has a role to play in the global economy. The modern spelling of ecology was first used in 1893.

TWO-WAY TRAFFIC
Many relationships between different species are far more complex than simply that of animal and food plant, or predator and prey. This bee is visiting the flowers of the heather in search of the nectar on which it feeds, but the plant benefits from the bee's visit too. The bee will carry away pollen from the flower on its body, and this pollen will fertilize other heather flowers as the bee continues its search. The nectar that attracts the bee ensures the survival of the plant. Such relationships are an important part of ecology.

Bee

Heather flower

A HIERARCHY OF COMPLEXITY
Living things can be studied at six different levels. First, there is the *individual*, a plant or an animal belonging to a particular species. A group of individuals of the same species is called a *population*. Different populations of species exist together in a *community*, and several different communities may be found together in a characteristic way, creating an *ecosystem*. Different ecosystems are found together in a single geographical zone, sharing the same climatic conditions and constituting a *biome* (as in the map below). All the Earth's varied biomes together make up the highest level of organization, the *biosphere*, the thin life-bearing layer that forms the outer surface of the planet.

Biosphere

Biome

Ecosystem

Community

Population

Individual

EARTH'S MAJOR LIFE ZONES
The planet's land surfaces can be divided into zones, or biomes, according to the climate and other physical factors in each area. Each biome has a distinctive combination of life forms that are able to thrive in the particular conditions found there, and each has a distinctive kind of vegetation. In this book, some of the major biomes are discussed, as well as some habitats that are distributed around the globe, such as coral reefs and fresh waters, which do not form continuous zones in themselves. Although many factors influence the locations of the biomes, this map reveals that latitude – distance from the equator – has a noticeable effect.

Mouse (prey)

- Tundra
- Temperate forest
- Savannah
- Temperate grassland
- Temperate rain forest
- Boreal forest
- Desert
- Tropical rain forest
- Mountain
- Scrubland

7

Nature's primary producers

Plants create their own food. For this reason, they are called autotrophic (self-feeding). They use pigments such as chlorophyll, the green pigment in leaves, to capture light energy, which they then turn into stored chemical energy to fuel their life processes. This two-stage process is called photosynthesis. Ecologists refer to plants as producers because they produce new living (organic) material from non-living (inorganic) materials. The rate at which energy is stored by plants is called the net primary productivity of the ecosystem. The Sun is the source of all this energy, but only a tiny fraction of the energy reaching this planet is actually used to create plant material.

About one-half is absorbed by the atmosphere. Only one-quarter of the rest is of the right wavelength for photosynthesis, and very little of this is actually converted into plant material. In grasslands, about 0.4 percent of the total incoming radiation ends up in net primary production. In forests this can reach 1 percent, while in the ocean it may be as low as 0.01 percent. All the energy entering an ecosystem is eventually released back into space as heat.

A MOSAIC OF LEAVES
In shape and form, leaves are adapted to the task of capturing light. Most leaves are broad in order to present as large an area to the light as possible. The surface layer of the leaf, the cuticle, is often matt rather than shiny, reducing the amount of light that it reflects. In many plants the leaves grow to form an interlocking mosaic, presenting an almost continuous surface to the light. By contrast, the leaves of some plants that live in intense light, such as the Australian eucalyptus, hang downward, to present the minimum surface area to the midday sun and reduce water loss.

ENERGY TRANSFORMATION
The surface of this car is covered with solar cells that convert light energy into electrical energy. This is used to run an electric motor and propel the car. Despite developments in this sophisticated technology, science is still a long way from being able to replicate photosynthesis.

BIOME	PRODUCTION
Extreme desert, rock, and ice	60
Desert scrub	1,320
Subsistence agriculture	1,528
Open ocean	2,420
Arctic and alpine tundra, and heathland	2,650
Continental shelf of oceans	6,620
Temperate grasslands	9,240
Lakes, rivers, and streams	9,450
Temperate woodland and scrub	11,340
Industrialized agriculture	12,290
Boreal coniferous forest	13,100
Tropical savanna	13,440
Temperate deciduous forest	22,210
Tropical swamps and marshes	35,280
Tropical estuaries and attached algae	35,280
Tropical rain forests	36,160

PRIMARY PRODUCTIVITY
Different biomes (p. 7) store energy, in the form of plant material, at different rates. This table shows the average annual net primary production in the world's major biomes, from the least productive (desert) to the most productive (tropical rain forest). The figures are given in units of kilojoules (kJ) per square meter (10 sq ft).

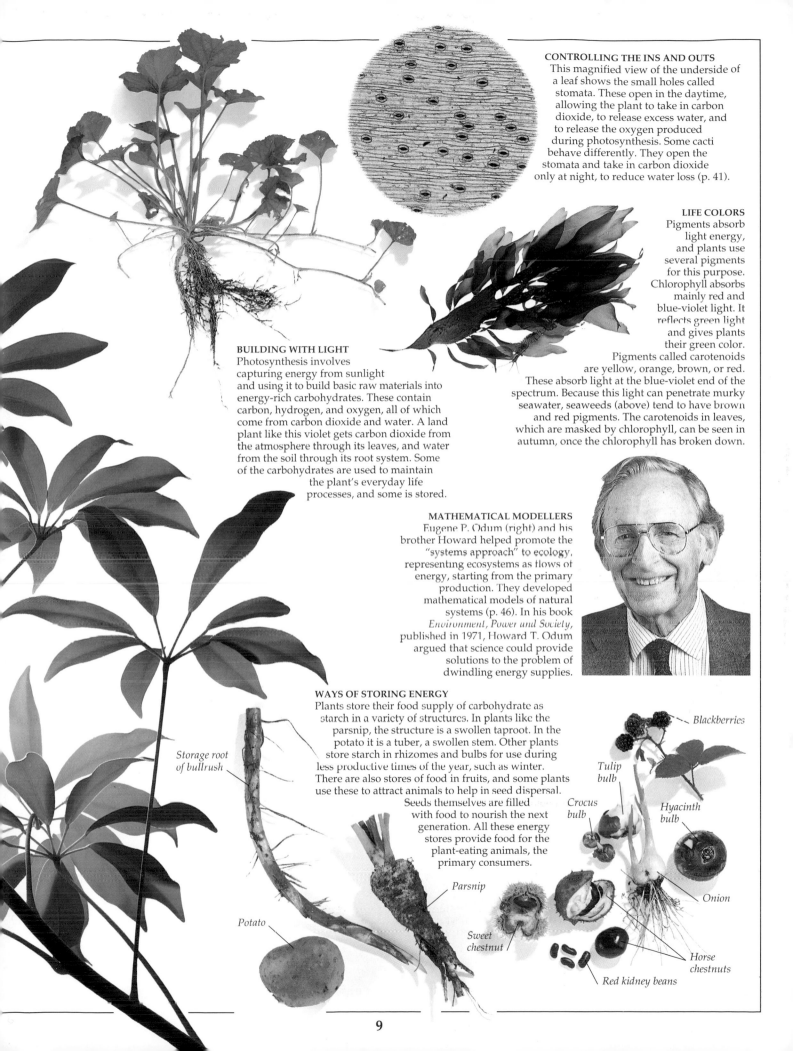

CONTROLLING THE INS AND OUTS
This magnified view of the underside of a leaf shows the small holes called stomata. These open in the daytime, allowing the plant to take in carbon dioxide, to release excess water, and to release the oxygen produced during photosynthesis. Some cacti behave differently. They open the stomata and take in carbon dioxide only at night, to reduce water loss (p. 41).

LIFE COLORS
Pigments absorb light energy, and plants use several pigments for this purpose. Chlorophyll absorbs mainly red and blue-violet light. It reflects green light and gives plants their green color. Pigments called carotenoids are yellow, orange, brown, or red. These absorb light at the blue-violet end of the spectrum. Because this light can penetrate murky seawater, seaweeds (above) tend to have brown and red pigments. The carotenoids in leaves, which are masked by chlorophyll, can be seen in autumn, once the chlorophyll has broken down.

BUILDING WITH LIGHT
Photosynthesis involves capturing energy from sunlight and using it to build basic raw materials into energy-rich carbohydrates. These contain carbon, hydrogen, and oxygen, all of which come from carbon dioxide and water. A land plant like this violet gets carbon dioxide from the atmosphere through its leaves, and water from the soil through its root system. Some of the carbohydrates are used to maintain the plant's everyday life processes, and some is stored.

MATHEMATICAL MODELLERS
Eugene P. Odum (right) and his brother Howard helped promote the "systems approach" to ecology, representing ecosystems as flows of energy, starting from the primary production. They developed mathematical models of natural systems (p. 46). In his book *Environment, Power and Society*, published in 1971, Howard T. Odum argued that science could provide solutions to the problem of dwindling energy supplies.

WAYS OF STORING ENERGY
Plants store their food supply of carbohydrate as starch in a variety of structures. In plants like the parsnip, the structure is a swollen taproot. In the potato it is a tuber, a swollen stem. Other plants store starch in rhizomes and bulbs for use during less productive times of the year, such as winter. There are also stores of food in fruits, and some plants use these to attract animals to help in seed dispersal. Seeds themselves are filled with food to nourish the next generation. All these energy stores provide food for the plant-eating animals, the primary consumers.

Storage root of bullrush

Blackberries

Tulip bulb

Crocus bulb

Hyacinth bulb

Parsnip

Onion

Potato

Sweet chestnut

Horse chestnuts

Red kidney beans

The transfer of energy

IN EVERY ECOSYSTEM, energy is trapped and stored by plants – the primary producers. Some of this energy is transferred to the animals that eat the plants. They are the primary consumers. Animals that eat other animals are known as secondary consumers, because they receive the energy from the plants second hand, via the primary consumers. In some circumstances, the secondary consumers are eaten by other predators – the tertiary, or third stage, consumers. Ecologists refer to each of these stages as a trophic level. At each stage, some energy is passed to the next level, where it is then stored as plant material or as the flesh of living animals. Some energy is always lost in the transfer from one trophic level to the next. The amount of living material in each trophic level is known as the standing crop, whether plant or animal, and this represents the amount of potential energy available to the next level. The size of the standing crop can be expressed as biomass (literally the mass), or as the numbers of plants and animals at each trophic level. Ecologists can use these figures to compare ecosystems and understand how they work.

Tawny owl – top predator

THE TROPHIC PYRAMID
The trophic levels in a particular ecosystem can be represented as a pyramid. The number of levels varies but, because energy is limited and there are energy losses at each level, there can rarely be more than six levels in any ecosystem. In this woodland pyramid, the owl is the top predator. It is both a secondary consumer, feeding on rodents such as voles and mice, and a tertiary consumer, because it also feeds on the weasels that prey on the small rodents. The rodents are primary consumers, eating plant material in the form of grasses, seeds, and berries.

Baby weasel

Juvenile weasel

Weasels – secondary consumers

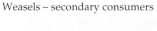

Bank vole

Yellow-necked woodmouse

Small rodents – primary consumers

Seeds

Grass seed heads

Plants – primary producers

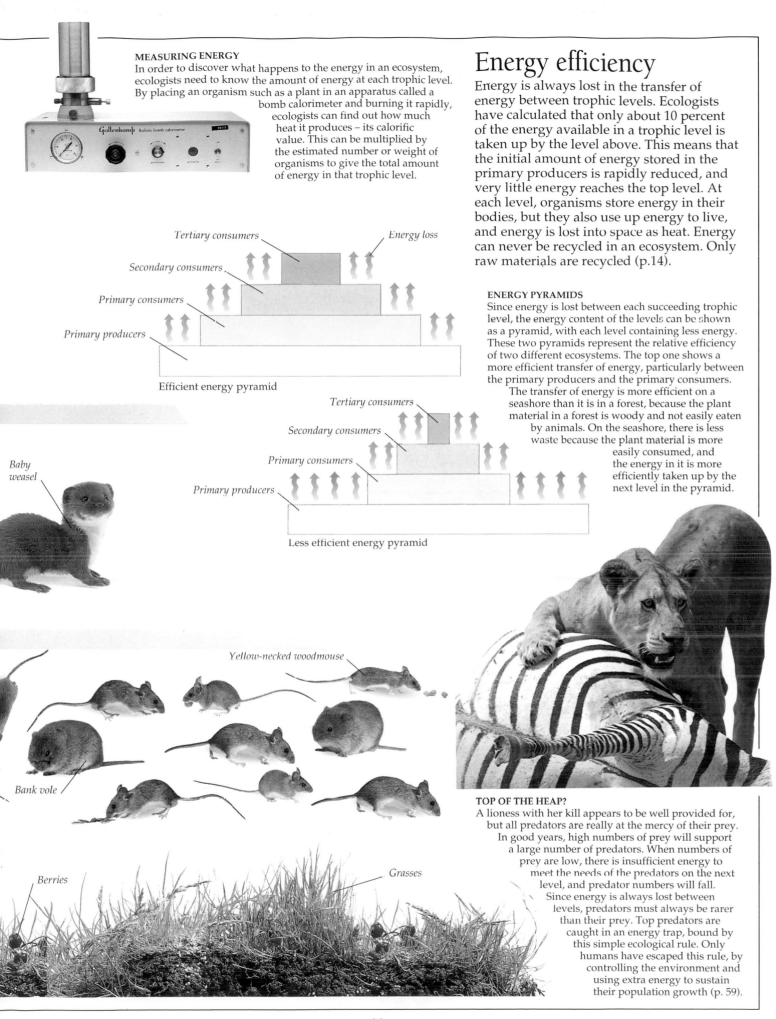

MEASURING ENERGY
In order to discover what happens to the energy in an ecosystem, ecologists need to know the amount of energy at each trophic level. By placing an organism such as a plant in an apparatus called a bomb calorimeter and burning it rapidly, ecologists can find out how much heat it produces – its calorific value. This can be multiplied by the estimated number or weight of organisms to give the total amount of energy in that trophic level.

Energy efficiency

Energy is always lost in the transfer of energy between trophic levels. Ecologists have calculated that only about 10 percent of the energy available in a trophic level is taken up by the level above. This means that the initial amount of energy stored in the primary producers is rapidly reduced, and very little energy reaches the top level. At each level, organisms store energy in their bodies, but they also use up energy to live, and energy is lost into space as heat. Energy can never be recycled in an ecosystem. Only raw materials are recycled (p.14).

ENERGY PYRAMIDS
Since energy is lost between each succeeding trophic level, the energy content of the levels can be shown as a pyramid, with each level containing less energy. These two pyramids represent the relative efficiency of two different ecosystems. The top one shows a more efficient transfer of energy, particularly between the primary producers and the primary consumers. The transfer of energy is more efficient on a seashore than it is in a forest, because the plant material in a forest is woody and not easily eaten by animals. On the seashore, there is less waste because the plant material is more easily consumed, and the energy in it is more efficiently taken up by the next level in the pyramid.

Tertiary consumers

Energy loss

Secondary consumers

Primary consumers

Primary producers

Efficient energy pyramid

Tertiary consumers

Secondary consumers

Primary consumers

Primary producers

Less efficient energy pyramid

Baby weasel

Yellow-necked woodmouse

Bank vole

Berries

Grasses

TOP OF THE HEAP?
A lioness with her kill appears to be well provided for, but all predators are really at the mercy of their prey. In good years, high numbers of prey will support a large number of predators. When numbers of prey are low, there is insufficient energy to meet the needs of the predators on the next level, and predator numbers will fall. Since energy is always lost between levels, predators must always be rarer than their prey. Top predators are caught in an energy trap, bound by this simple ecological rule. Only humans have escaped this rule, by controlling the environment and using extra energy to sustain their population growth (p. 59).

Food webs

FOR ECOLOGISTS TO UNDERSTAND how energy enters and passes through an ecosystem, they must understand the feeding relationships between the organisms in that ecosystem. The transfer of food energy from plants through repeated stages of eating and being eaten is known as a food chain. In a simple food chain, a plant is eaten by a plant eater (herbivore), which in its turn is eaten by a meat eater (carnivore). There are many food chains on this page, but because nature is complex the chains are highly interconnected, creating a food web. This ocean food web shows that many animals feed at several different trophic levels (p. 10). The herring gull, for example, feeds on a wide range of prey species.

KNOCK-ON EFFECT
The destruction of the large whales in the ocean around Antarctica led to an increase in the number of the shrimp-like krill on which they fed. This led in turn to rapid rises in the populations of other species, such as crabeater seals, which fed on the increasing krill. The removal of predator species created an opportunity for other species to thrive.

Common seal

Herring gull

Common lobster

Oystercatcher

Dog whelk

Shanny

Lugworm

Common mussel

Common prawn

INTRICATE WEB
Very few animals feed on just one other kind of animal. The risks of being dependent on one species are too great. This food web shows the range of food that different species eat. Arrows run from each species to the other organisms that feed on it. Even this fairly complicated web shows only some of the connections.

Plant and animal remains

Zooplankton

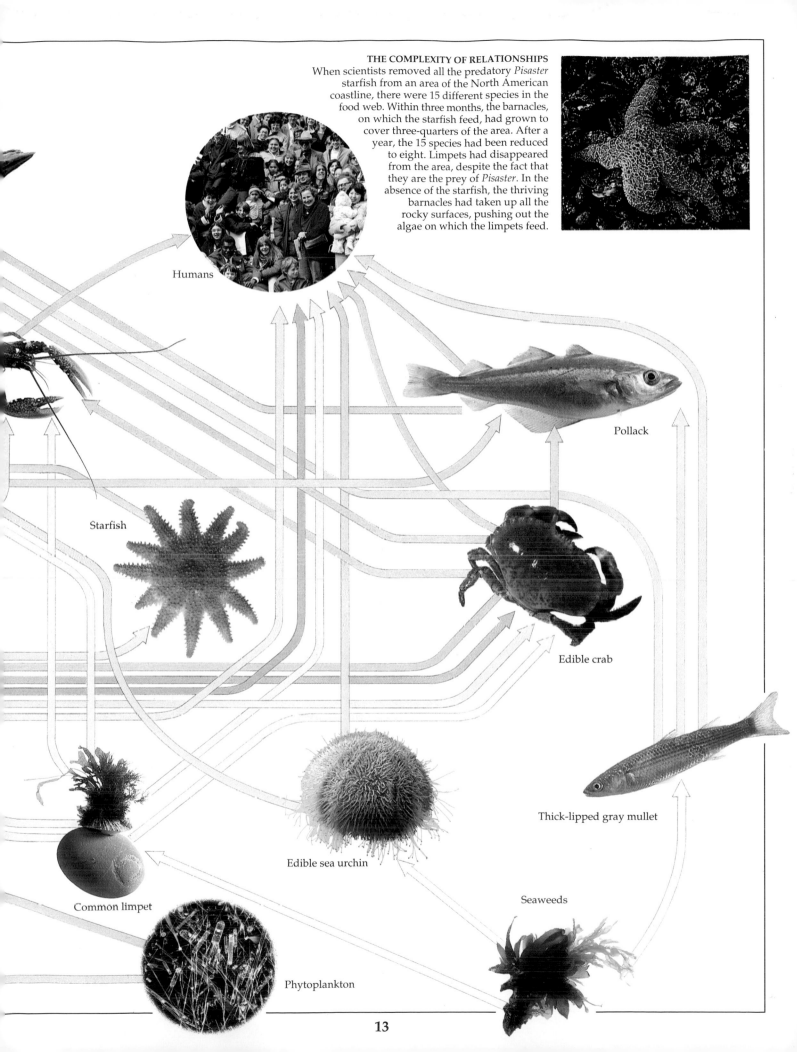

THE COMPLEXITY OF RELATIONSHIPS
When scientists removed all the predatory *Pisaster* starfish from an area of the North American coastline, there were 15 different species in the food web. Within three months, the barnacles, on which the starfish feed, had grown to cover three-quarters of the area. After a year, the 15 species had been reduced to eight. Limpets had disappeared from the area, despite the fact that they are the prey of *Pisaster*. In the absence of the starfish, the thriving barnacles had taken up all the rocky surfaces, pushing out the algae on which the limpets feed.

Humans

Pollack

Starfish

Edible crab

Thick-lipped gray mullet

Common limpet

Edible sea urchin

Seaweeds

Phytoplankton

Recycling to live

A<small>LL LIVING THINGS</small> die eventually. In ecological terms, the chemicals of which living things are made are borrowed from the Earth, and at death they are returned. All the material that every animal, from the smallest fly to the largest elephant, takes in as food also returns to the Earth, as waste matter. The dead material and waste matter form the diet of a group of living organisms called decomposers. They include a range of bacteria, fungi, and small animals that break down nature's wastes into ever smaller pieces until all the chemicals are released into the air, the soil, and the water, making them available to other living things. Without the carbon dioxide that decomposition releases, all plant life would die out. Without the oxygen that plants give out, and without the food that they supply, life would grind to a halt and all animals would starve. The decomposers are a vital link in the natural cycle of life and death.

Worm

WORKING UNDERGROUND
Worms play a particularly important role in the process of decomposition on land. At the surface they eat dead leaves. These are then carried down into the soil. The digested material is passed out as droppings, and these are consumed by fungi and bacteria, ensuring complete recycling of the leaf litter. Worms also turn the soil over, supplying it with oxygen and bringing material from lower levels up to the surface. Worms therefore have an important effect on soil fertility. In temperate soils, each square meter (10 sq ft) of topsoil may contain as many as 700 worms.

Rotting wood

SLUGS AND SNAILS
Although both slugs and snails feed on living plants, as gardeners know to their cost, decomposing plant material also makes up a large proportion of their diet. They rasp away at the plant fibers with their rough "tongue," called a radula. This breaks up the material and draws it into the mouth. Slugs and snails produce the enzyme cellulase, and this enables them to digest cellulose, the main component of all plants. Their droppings then become available to fungi and bacteria. Some species of slug are particularly fond of other animals' droppings and will even eat dog dung.

Slug

Worm

Woodlouse

HARD TO BREAK DOWN
Much of the waste and dead plant material, such as the twigs and stems below, consists of cellulose. The pages of this book are made mainly from cellulose fibers derived from plants, usually from trees. Like sugar or bread, cellulose is a carbohydrate. It contains the essential carbon that all living things need. However, only a very few organisms are capable of breaking it down and using it. The main decomposers of cellulose are bacteria, some of which live inside the guts of other animals, and fungi, such as the kinds known as smuts and rusts that grow on plants.

Small twigs and pieces of bark

DETRITIVORES
In every ecosystem, there is always waste material, consisting of dead plant material, animal waste and droppings, and dead animals. Collectively this is called detritus. The larger animals that are able to tackle this material directly are called detritivores. These organisms are able to digest quite large pieces of detritus and turn this into their own droppings. This renders the material more easily digested by smaller decomposers such as fungi and bacteria, which break it down even further into simple chemicals. Some of the most familiar detritivores are woodlice, worms, slugs (left) and snails, millipedes, and springtails.

Slug

Centipede

INVISIBLE ROTTERS
Bacteria, microscopically small organisms that are invisible to the naked eye, are normally associated with diseases, but they are also important in decomposition. When they occur in vast numbers, they can form colored patches, for example, on leaf litter in woods. They do well in moist or wet conditions (where bacterial cells can grow quickly), and some grow in anaerobic conditions, where there is little oxygen (preventing fungi from competing). Like fungi, bacteria produce enzymes to digest the waste material, so that their cells can absorb it.

DEATH ON THE THAMES

This cartoon was published in 1854 in a London magazine, when the smell from the pollution of the Thames River in England reached such a state that Parliament had to be abandoned. All the city's human waste was being thrown into the water, where decomposition used up all the oxygen and caused the death of all life in the river. Parliament was forced to find money for the construction of drains and a sewage treatment plant.

Slug

MODERN METHODS

Today the same basic system of sewage treatment is found throughout the world. Natural decomposers are put to good use. The sewage is passed over beds of bacteria and protozoa that break down the organic content of the waste into its constituent chemicals. These can then be removed from the liquid, leaving the water in a much cleaner state, free from organic material.

ARMORED WOOD EATERS

Woodlice, members of the crab and lobster group, survive only in moist conditions. They play a particularly important role in the decomposition of dead plant material, which they eat and convert into droppings.

Woodlouse

Fruiting body of fungus

Dead twig being broken down by saprotrophic fungus

Energy and material

FEEDING FUNGI

The part of the fungus that is visible on wood or above the ground is its fruiting body, the part involved in reproduction. There are several fruiting bodies on this twig, but this is only part of the fungus. Within the wood there is a network of tiny threads called hyphae, and these take in food. They dissolve the cellulose, using the enzyme cellulase. The fungus then absorbs this pre-digested soup through the hyphae. Bacteria also feed on dead material in this way – a feeding method known as saprotrophic nutrition.

DECOMPOSITION CYCLE

The arrows in this diagram show the flow of both energy and material in a forest. Leaf litter, composed of leaves, twigs, and branches, falls to the forest floor, where it becomes food for detritivores such as worms, and for fungi and bacteria. Dead detritivores are eaten by others of the same group. Most of the energy is finally lost to outer space in the form of heat from respiration and other bodily processes. Some is taken up by predators like the mole, which eats worms. When the mole dies, some of its energy passes to the decomposers. It has been estimated that about 90 percent of all primary production in an ecosystem passes through the decomposition cycle.

Leaf litter

Death

Feces

Detritivores

Fungi and bacteria

Predators

Death

Heat

Respiration and other metabolic processes

Respiration and other metabolic processes

Energy lost into space

DISSOLVING THE GLUE

Besides cellulose, wood contains a substance called lignin, which makes up about 30 percent of the material. Lignin acts like glue, binding the strands of cellulose together and giving wood additional strength. Like cellulose, it contains carbon; it too is difficult to break down. Some fungi are able to do this. They include the white and brown rots that cause conditions called wet rot and dry rot in wood.

Twigs and fungal spores

Spore print

Colony of microscopic yellow fungi

Colony of microscopic black fungi

MUSHROOM SPORES

This circular brown stain (right) was made by spores falling from the underside of a toadstool cap. The spores are the equivalent of a plant's seeds. They are dispersed by the wind. If, when they land, they come in contact with a source of nutrients, they will germinate, growing hyphae that spread through the food source and decompose it.

The water cycle

IN THE BIOSPHERE, energy flows in and out, but the chemicals essential for life processes are limited. They must be constantly recycled. Water is the most common compound on Earth, and all life on this planet depends on it to a greater or lesser extent. Water plays a vital role in the structure of living things (70 percent of our body weight is made up of water), but its most important quality is that many chemicals will dissolve in it. Plants need water in order to take in dissolved minerals through their roots. Animals rely on water in their lung tissues to absorb oxygen from the atmosphere. However, because it is a solvent, water is very vulnerable to pollution. Many manufactured chemicals, including very highly toxic poisons, can enter the water cycle at a variety of points and then be carried through the environment. The most serious pollutants are those that do not biodegrade or break down through natural processes. They can be taken up by plants and animals and can accumulate in animals at the top of the food chain (p. 61).

POLAR ICE
Much of the world's fresh water is actually locked up as ice at the North Pole, where it is mainly sea ice, and on land in Antarctica, as an ice sheet up to 1.86 miles (3 km) thick. Global warming (p. 19) may result in some of the ice melting, raising the sea level and flooding many low-lying areas of land.

LIFEBLOOD OF THE PLANET
Falling rain provides an essential link in one of nature's most important cycles by redistributing the moisture that has evaporated from land and sea. In this way, the water is made available once again for the life processes on which all animals and plants depend. On average, every water molecule passes through this cycle every 10 to 15 days, though molecules can remain in the ocean for up to 1,500 years.

THE KIDNEYS OF THE RIVER SYSTEM
Wetlands are low-lying areas through which rivers spread out and run slowly. They are important, as they hold onto water and act as a buffer when rainfall is low. Much of a river's sediment is deposited here, so wetlands are very productive and attract a rich diversity of wildlife. Wetlands are also a natural filter, extracting many of the pollutants that enter a river from industry and other human activities. Despite their importance, wetlands are constantly being destroyed as land is drained and reclaimed for human use.

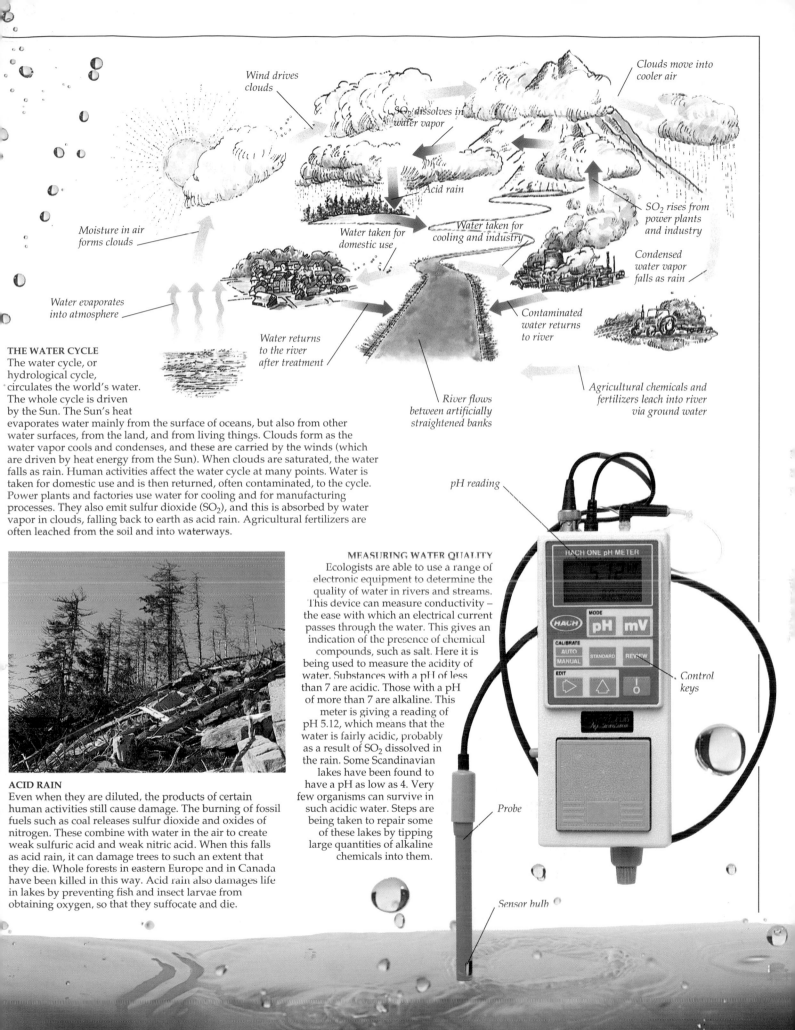

Wind drives clouds

Clouds move into cooler air

SO_2 dissolves in water vapor

Acid rain

SO_2 rises from power plants and industry

Moisture in air forms clouds

Water taken for domestic use

Water taken for cooling and industry

Condensed water vapor falls as rain

Water evaporates into atmosphere

Water returns to the river after treatment

Contaminated water returns to river

River flows between artificially straightened banks

Agricultural chemicals and fertilizers leach into river via ground water

THE WATER CYCLE

The water cycle, or hydrological cycle, circulates the world's water. The whole cycle is driven by the Sun. The Sun's heat evaporates water mainly from the surface of oceans, but also from other water surfaces, from the land, and from living things. Clouds form as the water vapor cools and condenses, and these are carried by the winds (which are driven by heat energy from the Sun). When clouds are saturated, the water falls as rain. Human activities affect the water cycle at many points. Water is taken for domestic use and is then returned, often contaminated, to the cycle. Power plants and factories use water for cooling and for manufacturing processes. They also emit sulfur dioxide (SO_2), and this is absorbed by water vapor in clouds, falling back to earth as acid rain. Agricultural fertilizers are often leached from the soil and into waterways.

ACID RAIN

Even when they are diluted, the products of certain human activities still cause damage. The burning of fossil fuels such as coal releases sulfur dioxide and oxides of nitrogen. These combine with water in the air to create weak sulfuric acid and weak nitric acid. When this falls as acid rain, it can damage trees to such an extent that they die. Whole forests in eastern Europe and in Canada have been killed in this way. Acid rain also damages life in lakes by preventing fish and insect larvae from obtaining oxygen, so that they suffocate and die.

MEASURING WATER QUALITY

Ecologists are able to use a range of electronic equipment to determine the quality of water in rivers and streams. This device can measure conductivity – the ease with which an electrical current passes through the water. This gives an indication of the presence of chemical compounds, such as salt. Here it is being used to measure the acidity of water. Substances with a pH of less than 7 are acidic. Those with a pH of more than 7 are alkaline. This meter is giving a reading of pH 5.12, which means that the water is fairly acidic, probably as a result of SO_2 dissolved in the rain. Some Scandinavian lakes have been found to have a pH as low as 4. Very few organisms can survive in such acidic water. Steps are being taken to repair some of these lakes by tipping large quantities of alkaline chemicals into them.

pH reading

HACH ONE pH METER

MODE
pH   mV

CALIBRATE
AUTO
MANUAL
STANDARD   REVIEW

EDIT

Control keys

Probe

Sensor bulb

Carbon on the move

ALL LIFE ON EARTH is based on the element carbon. It is constantly being passed between different parts of the biosphere in various chemical forms. It is found in the bodies of all living things, in the oceans, in the air, and in the Earth itself. In the atmosphere, when combined with oxygen, it forms carbon dioxide (CO_2). In plants, it becomes carbohydrate, the source of energy for plants and eventually for the animals that eat them. In the ground, and in the bones and shells of animals, carbon is found in the form of chalky calcium carbonate. Plants are the main point of exchange, converting atmospheric carbon dioxide into carbohydrate through photosynthesis (p. 8). Decomposition (p. 14) eventually returns all the carbon to the atmosphere.

UP IN SMOKE
As plants grow, they absorb carbon from the atmosphere. Some of it fuels the life processes of the plant, and some is incorporated into the structure of the plant, for example in cellulose. Every tree trunk is a store of carbon. When the tree is burned, this carbon is released back into the atmosphere as carbon dioxide.

CARBON CYCLE

Of all the carbon on Earth, less than 1 percent is in active circulation in the biosphere. The remainder is locked up as inorganic carbon in rocks and as organic carbon in fossil fuels (coal and oil). Growing plants take in carbon from the atmosphere (in the form of CO_2) and incorporate this in solid compounds in their structure. In this form, carbon passes into the food chains. Different ecosystems take up carbon at different rates. In a tropical rain forest, where plants grow quickly, carbon is incorporated at a rate that is 100 times greater than in a desert.

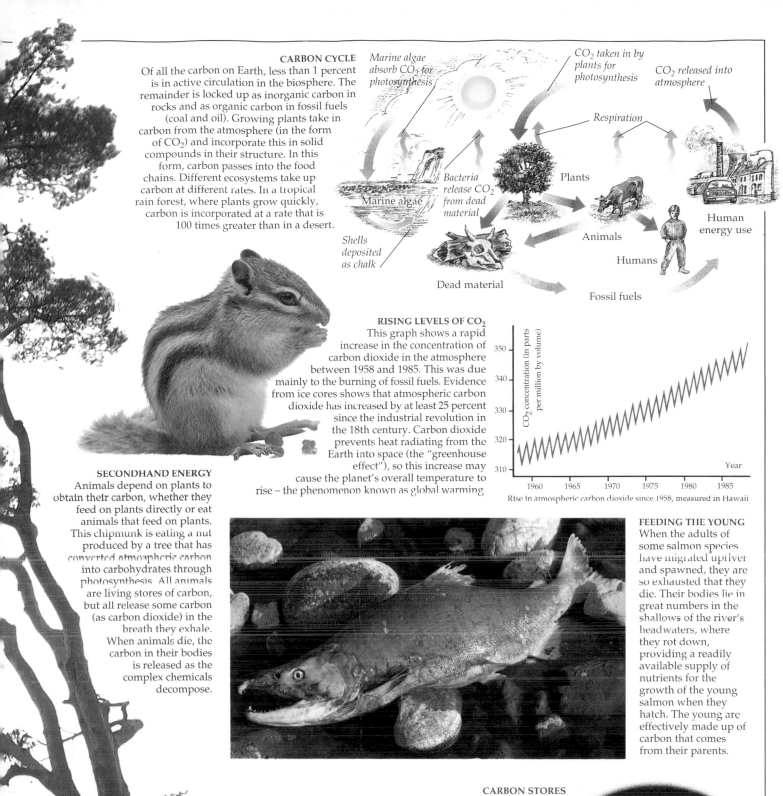

Marine algae absorb CO_2 for photosynthesis

CO_2 taken in by plants for photosynthesis

CO_2 released into atmosphere

Respiration

Bacteria release CO_2 from dead material

Marine algae

Plants

Human energy use

Shells deposited as chalk

Animals

Humans

Dead material

Fossil fuels

SECONDHAND ENERGY

Animals depend on plants to obtain their carbon, whether they feed on plants directly or eat animals that feed on plants. This chipmunk is eating a nut produced by a tree that has converted atmospheric carbon into carbohydrates through photosynthesis. All animals are living stores of carbon, but all release some carbon (as carbon dioxide) in the breath they exhale. When animals die, the carbon in their bodies is released as the complex chemicals decompose.

RISING LEVELS OF CO_2

This graph shows a rapid increase in the concentration of carbon dioxide in the atmosphere between 1958 and 1985. This was due mainly to the burning of fossil fuels. Evidence from ice cores shows that atmospheric carbon dioxide has increased by at least 25 percent since the industrial revolution in the 18th century. Carbon dioxide prevents heat radiating from the Earth into space (the "greenhouse effect"), so this increase may cause the planet's overall temperature to rise – the phenomenon known as global warming.

Rise in atmospheric carbon dioxide since 1958, measured in Hawaii

FEEDING THE YOUNG

When the adults of some salmon species have migrated upriver and spawned, they are so exhausted that they die. Their bodies lie in great numbers in the shallows of the river's headwaters, where they rot down, providing a readily available supply of nutrients for the growth of the young salmon when they hatch. The young are effectively made up of carbon that comes from their parents.

CARBON STORES

Carbon becomes locked up in the remains of animals and plants that fail to decompose completely – for example, in conditions of insufficient oxygen. In the shallow swamps of the Carboniferous period, which ended some 280 million years ago, trees and other plants died in just such conditions, forming thick layers. Over millions of years, the heat of the Earth and the pressure of material building up above them turned the carbon in these plants into coal. In a similar way, heat and pressure turned vast deposits of minute dead sea creatures, like these seen under a microscope, into a liquid store of carbon – oil. When these "fossil fuels" are burned, this carbon is released into the atmosphere. It has been estimated that there may be 50 times as much carbon locked up in the Earth's coal and oil as there is in all the living organisms in the world.

Keeping the Earth fertile

NITROGEN IS ONE OF THE INGREDIENTS of protein and DNA. As such it is an essential element in the structure of all living things. Although gaseous nitrogen makes up 78 percent of the Earth's atmosphere, plants and animals cannot use it in this form. It is the nitrogen cycle, in which microscopic bacteria transform nitrogen into a variety of compounds, that makes nitrogen available to other living things. Bacteria described as "nitrogen-fixing" can convert nitrogen in the air directly into nitrates in the soil. Nitrates are soluble in water, and plants are able to take them up through their roots. In turn, animals obtain their nitrogen from plants. The protein in waste material, such as dung or dead plants and animals, also contains nitrogen. Various bacteria break down the protein and finally convert the nitrogen into nitrates, which can be used by other organisms. Some of the nitrates are taken up by plants, and some complete the cycle when they are changed back to nitrogen gas by yet another kind of bacteria.

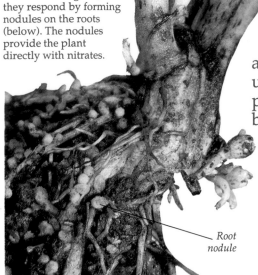

A HUMBLE DIET
A dung fly digesting manure begins the process of breaking down protein and releasing the nitrogen compounds in it.

NITROGEN FIXER
A vital supply of usable nitrogen comes from the nitrogen-fixing bacteria *Rhizobium* that associate with plants called legumes, such as peas, beans, and clover. A chemical in the roots encourages the bacteria to grow, and they respond by forming nodules on the roots (below). The nodules provide the plant directly with nitrates.

Root nodule

ENRICHING THE SOIL
A rotting cowpat is a point of transformation in the nitrogen cycle. Dung contains large amounts of nitrogen locked up in the proteins that the animal has eaten as plant material. Various bacteria release this nitrogen by breaking down the protein into ever simpler compounds, and finally into nitrates, which plants can take up through their roots. For this reason, the grass around a cowpat is often more lush than the surrounding vegetation.

TOO MUCH OF A GOOD THING
In order to improve the productivity of land and to increase crop yields, farmers in developed countries use enormous quantities of artificially produced nitrates as agricultural fertilizers. There is now growing evidence that these additional nitrates are overloading the natural system. Before they can be broken down or converted into atmospheric nitrogen, they are often leached out of the soil by rain. These dissolved nitrates are then carried into streams and river systems, and down into ground water. In some parts of the world, water for domestic use contains such high concentrations of nitrates that it exceeds safety levels for human consumption.

TRANSFORMING AN ESSENTIAL ELEMENT

The cycling of nitrogen involves a sequence of transformations. Gaseous nitrogen is "fixed" – turned into ammonia and then into nitrates that can be absorbed by plants – by bacteria in soil and in the root nodules of particular kinds of plants. These nitrates are then taken up by plants. Animals eat plants and use some of the complex nitrogen compounds. Nitrogen in dead animals and manure is converted into nitrites by the nitrifying bacterium *Nitrosomonas*. *Nitrobacter* bacteria convert nitrites to nitrates. The rain leaches some of this into the soil, some is taken up by plants, and denitrifying bacteria release some into the atmosphere as nitrogen gas. Lightning changes atmospheric nitrogen into nitrogen dioxide, which is soluble in water. The rain carries it into the soil as weak nitric acid.

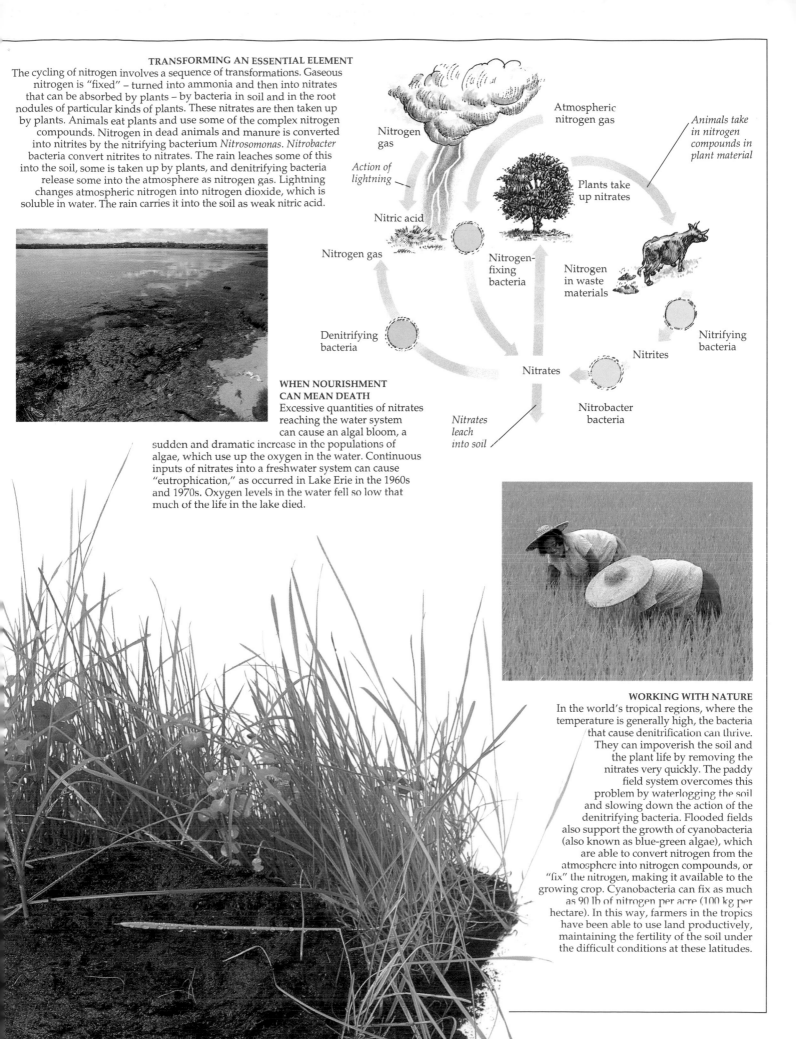

Nitrogen gas

Atmospheric nitrogen gas

Animals take in nitrogen compounds in plant material

Action of lightning

Plants take up nitrates

Nitric acid

Nitrogen gas

Nitrogen-fixing bacteria

Nitrogen in waste materials

Denitrifying bacteria

Nitrifying bacteria

Nitrites

Nitrates

Nitrates leach into soil

Nitrobacter bacteria

WHEN NOURISHMENT CAN MEAN DEATH

Excessive quantities of nitrates reaching the water system can cause an algal bloom, a sudden and dramatic increase in the populations of algae, which use up the oxygen in the water. Continuous inputs of nitrates into a freshwater system can cause "eutrophication," as occurred in Lake Erie in the 1960s and 1970s. Oxygen levels in the water fell so low that much of the life in the lake died.

WORKING WITH NATURE

In the world's tropical regions, where the temperature is generally high, the bacteria that cause denitrification can thrive. They can impoverish the soil and the plant life by removing the nitrates very quickly. The paddy field system overcomes this problem by waterlogging the soil and slowing down the action of the denitrifying bacteria. Flooded fields also support the growth of cyanobacteria (also known as blue-green algae), which are able to convert nitrogen from the atmosphere into nitrogen compounds, or "fix" the nitrogen, making it available to the growing crop. Cyanobacteria can fix as much as 90 lb of nitrogen per acre (100 kg per hectare). In this way, farmers in the tropics have been able to use land productively, maintaining the fertility of the soil under the difficult conditions at these latitudes.

The life-giving soil

THE SOILS ON WHICH PLANTS DEPEND are created by the interaction of living and nonliving parts of the environment. Their composition is influenced by five main factors: climate and weathering; geology – the underlying rocks; topography – for example, whether the land slopes or is near a river; the action of living things, including humans; and time. Soil has six main components: mineral particles, including silt, clay, and sand; humus – mainly organic material that forms a thin film around each crumb of soil; nutrient ions, such as calcium and potassium; water; air between the soil particles; and living organisms, such as worms and microscopic life. These factors all influence the fertility of the soil. Soils can be studied by digging down and creating a soil profile. The three main layers are the topsoil, the subsoil, and the parent material. New soil is continuously being formed, but soil is being eroded almost twice as fast, often as a result of human activities, such as the destruction of the rain forest and poor agricultural practices.

MONUMENTAL FAILURE?
Some ecologists think that soil erosion caused the end of civilization on Easter Island, off the coast of Chile. It may be that when the trees on the island were cut down, possibly to help in the construction and movement of the famous stone heads, the rains washed away the nutrients from the soil, and then the soil itself. Sufficient food could no longer be grown, and the people were finally forced to leave the island altogether.

Heather and other acid-resistant plants

Highly organic acidic topsoil

Stony layer

Subsoil colored by leached minerals

ACIDIC HEATHLAND
The heathland soil is sandy and fairly dry. The thin layer of plant debris tends to be acidic. Worms and microbes cannot tolerate these conditions, so decomposition is very slow, and the dry soil is poor in nutrients. The acid leaches into the subsoil, as do minerals such as iron, which gives the lower layers an orange color.

Rich plant growth

Plant roots extending deep into soil

Thick layer of rich and fertile topsoil

FARMS AND GARDENS
A profile through a vegetable garden shows a thick rich topsoil, created by long-term human management. Continual digging and the regular addition of compost or manure produces a well drained and well-aerated soil with a high organic content. This kind of soil is very fertile and is likely to support a large number of earthworms.

Bilberry plants

Thin acidic peaty layer

Subsoil of shale and slate stained with organic material

WET MOORLAND
Below the moorland soil lie non-porous shales and slate. Some of this rock is seen in the subsoil. Rainfall here is far higher than on the heathland, keeping the top layer wet. As water runs off, it carries away the soluble nutrients. Particles of organic material from dead plant remains build up to form an acidic peaty layer.

Indicator paper showing pH of 8

Chalky downland soil

Indicator paper showing pH of 7

Cultivated garden soil

Indicator paper showing pH of 5

Heathland soil

Neutral

7   8

6   9

5   Color scale of increasing pH   10

3   12

1   14

Highly acidic   Highly alkaline

SOIL CHEMISTRY

Soils differ widely in their chemical composition, affecting the kinds of plants that will grow in them. In this simple chemical test, indicator paper is dipped into a solution of the soil to measure acidity and alkalinity. Chalky soil (top) has a pH of about 8 (slightly alkaline). With a pH of 7, the garden soil is neutral, and the heathland soil is distinctly acid, with a pH of about 5.

Organic material

Suspended clay particles

Silt

Sand

SEPARATING MATTER

A simple analysis of soil composition begins with the separation of some of the solid material present. This can be done by mixing some soil in a beaker full of water and then shaking it up. Organic material, or humus, tends to float to the top. The most dense particles, such as sand, sink to the very bottom. A layer of lighter particles, such as silt, forms on top of this. Tiny particles of clay settle to the bottom very slowly. The relative amounts of each of these constituents depend on the kind of soil.

FILTERING OUT THE LIVING

Many of the living organisms in the ground are extremely small and difficult to detect, but they are a vital ingredient in the soil. This apparatus, called a Tullgren funnel after the scientist who designed it, is used by ecologists to collect and identify those tiny organisms. Soil is placed on a fine mesh in the top of the funnel, and a light source is placed over the apparatus. Small creatures move away from the light, making their way down through the mesh. They then fall down the funnel and into a vial containing alcohol to preserve them. These animals, which include springtails, nematode worms, mites, and many others, can then be studied under a microscope.

Soil sample

Fine mesh

Glass funnel

Clamp

Vial

Small animals

Alcohol solution

Silt and small animals

Glacier

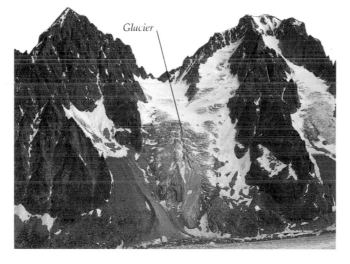

GRINDING UP THE ROCKS

Much of the world's soil is derived from rock that has been worn down by physical erosion – for example, by glaciers that grind up the rock under them. Glaciers also transport this soil, called glacial till, to new areas where it creates new ecological conditions. Soil can be created by the action of water freezing in cracks and crevices, expanding and splitting the rock. Water and wind erode rock and break it into smaller pieces. Plants such as lichens and mosses grow on rocks and chemically erode them into smaller particles. These then combine with organic material to make soil.

THE PRICE OF LOST SOIL

Soil acts like a natural sponge, absorbing water and releasing it slowly. In the Himalayas, much of the forest that holds the soil onto the steep mountain sides has been cut down for firewood. This has allowed the soils to be washed away by the monsoon rains, into the rivers and down to the sea. As a result, when the rains come, the water that would have been absorbed by the soil rushes down the rocky slopes and into the rivers, swelling them and flooding lowland towns and villages, causing untold death and damage. Countries such as Bangladesh suffer frequent flooding.

The distribution of life

ALTHOUGH LIFE MAY APPEAR to be uniformly distributed over the surface of the Earth, in reality it is very uneven. In some desert areas, and in parts of the frozen continent of Antarctica, no living things can tolerate the tough physical conditions. There seems to be life throughout the oceans, but where there are no currents to bring essential nutrients, the waters are virtually dead, because plants need more than just sunlight to live. On a smaller scale, the two sides of a valley, or of a tree, may be home to very different kinds of organisms if the two sides receive unequal amounts of sunlight or rain. When ecologists study the distribution of organisms, they try to discover the physical and biological factors that influence the presence or absence of particular species. They also look for any historical factors that may have affected where species are found, and for patterns that might indicate how the distribution of populations could change in the future. This is especially important in the case of rare or endangered species.

RING-TAILED CASTAWAY
The distribution of lemurs is extremely limited. These unique primates are found only on the large island of Madagascar, off the east coast of Africa. Fossil evidence shows that the lemurs, including a giant species, were once much more widespread than they are today. The separation of the island from the mainland has allowed them, and some other species, to evolve and exploit an entire range of unoccupied ecological niches. Had Madagascar remained connected to the African mainland, the lemurs there would probably have died out for the same unknown reasons that they did elsewhere.

TWO SIDES – TWO WORLDS
The contrast between opposite sides of a tree provides a vivid example of species distribution. On the side where the Sun keeps the bark hot and dry, the surface of the tree appears to be virtually lifeless, because conditions prevent plants from establishing themselves. On the side facing away from the Sun, where the bark remains cool and moist, the tree is covered with a thick growth of organisms, such as algae, lichens, ivy, and even moss, that thrive in these conditions.

Bare bark on side of tree facing the Sun

SAMPLING THE SEABED
Faced with the impossibility of counting all the individuals, or even all the species, in a large area, ecologists use a sampling method to find out more about the distribution of organisms. A square frame of known size, called a quadrat, is placed on the surface of the ground (or in this case the seabed) and the number of species and individuals within it are counted. This is repeated several times, and the data can be used to look for patterns of distribution. Such sampling methods are a common tool in ecological population studies.

Quadrat

Distribution of four species of winkle down the seashore

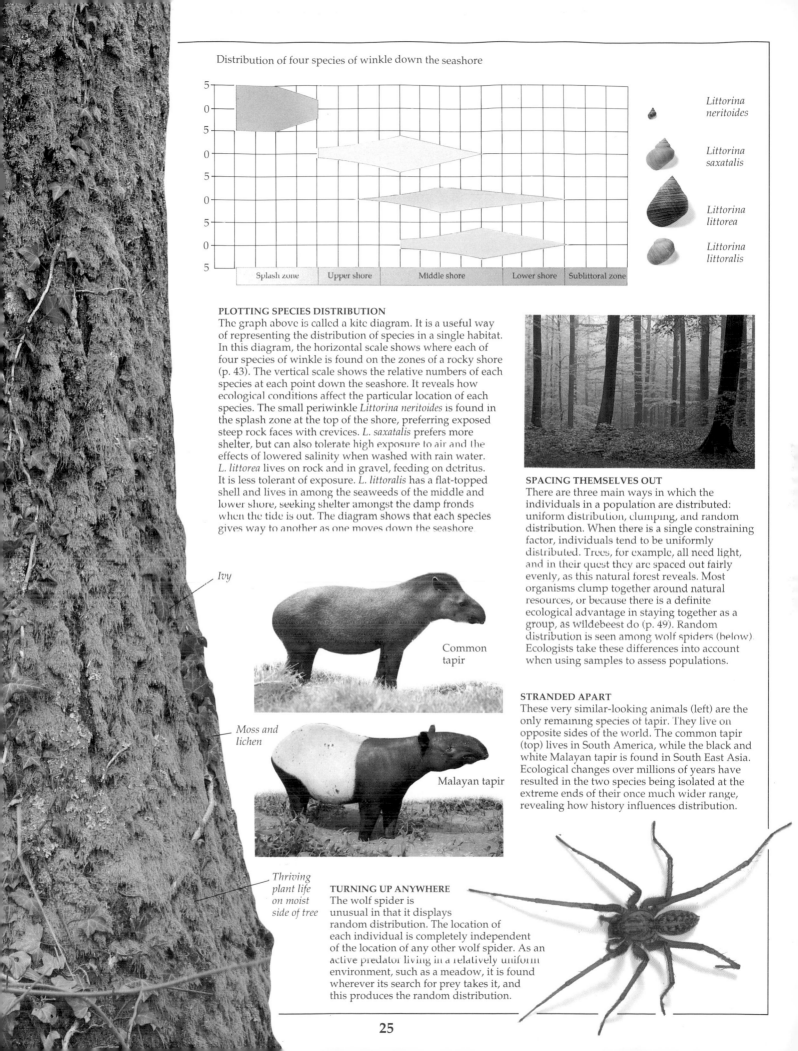

| | Splash zone | Upper shore | Middle shore | Lower shore | Sublittoral zone |

Littorina neritoides

Littorina saxatalis

Littorina littorea

Littorina littoralis

PLOTTING SPECIES DISTRIBUTION
The graph above is called a kite diagram. It is a useful way of representing the distribution of species in a single habitat. In this diagram, the horizontal scale shows where each of four species of winkle is found on the zones of a rocky shore (p. 43). The vertical scale shows the relative numbers of each species at each point down the seashore. It reveals how ecological conditions affect the particular location of each species. The small periwinkle *Littorina neritoides* is found in the splash zone at the top of the shore, preferring exposed steep rock faces with crevices. *L. saxatalis* prefers more shelter, but can also tolerate high exposure to air and the effects of lowered salinity when washed with rain water. *L. littorea* lives on rock and in gravel, feeding on detritus. It is less tolerant of exposure. *L. littoralis* has a flat-topped shell and lives in among the seaweeds of the middle and lower shore, seeking shelter amongst the damp fronds when the tide is out. The diagram shows that each species gives way to another as one moves down the seashore.

SPACING THEMSELVES OUT
There are three main ways in which the individuals in a population are distributed: uniform distribution, clumping, and random distribution. When there is a single constraining factor, individuals tend to be uniformly distributed. Trees, for example, all need light, and in their quest they are spaced out fairly evenly, as this natural forest reveals. Most organisms clump together around natural resources, or because there is a definite ecological advantage in staying together as a group, as wildebeest do (p. 49). Random distribution is seen among wolf spiders (below). Ecologists take these differences into account when using samples to assess populations.

Ivy

Common tapir

Moss and lichen

Malayan tapir

STRANDED APART
These very similar-looking animals (left) are the only remaining species of tapir. They live on opposite sides of the world. The common tapir (top) lives in South America, while the black and white Malayan tapir is found in South East Asia. Ecological changes over millions of years have resulted in the two species being isolated at the extreme ends of their once much wider range, revealing how history influences distribution.

Thriving plant life on moist side of tree

TURNING UP ANYWHERE
The wolf spider is unusual in that it displays random distribution. The location of each individual is completely independent of the location of any other wolf spider. As an active predator living in a relatively uniform environment, such as a meadow, it is found wherever its search for prey takes it, and this produces the random distribution.

Ecological niche

IN ORDER TO UNDERSTAND a person, it is necessary to know more than just their address. How do they spend their time? What are their interests? Most importantly, how do they fit into the community and relate to its other members? The same questions can be asked about other living organisms. If the address is the habitat of an animal or plant, the place where it lives, then its activities and all the other factors are its ecological niche. Charles Elton was one of the first ecologists to describe an ecological niche in terms of the "functional status of an organism in its community." In this sense, the term niche means the way in which a species uses the available resources to survive, and the ways in which its existence affects the other organisms living around it. Laboratory experiments and observation of the natural world have led to the discovery that most species occupy different ecological niches. It is believed that this is to avoid competition between species when resources are limited. If two species were in direct competition, one of them would inevitably become extinct or would have to seek an alternative niche.

Strong pointed bill

Nuts and seeds

Greenfinch

Short strong bill

Buds of fruit trees

Bullfinch

Upper and lower parts of bill cross each other

Pine cones

Crossbill

A COLONIZING NICHE
Stinging nettles thrive close to old human settlements, dung heaps, rabbit warrens, and seabird colonies. Why are these all ideal habitats for the nettle? The answer lies in the soil. The nettle's niche is as a colonizer of phosphate-rich soils, which are found in all these habitats because of the waste organic material that has been deposited. The nettles rapidly spread over a large area, excluding all other plants. Once the phosphates are used up, the habitat is no longer ideal for nettles, and other plants move into the area.

DIVIDING UP RESOURCES
Some groups of closely related animals are able to occupy the same geographical space without directly competing for the same resources, because they exploit different niches, particularly different food sources. The very different bills of these three species of finch reveal the foods that they eat and show their ecological preferences. The greenfinch (top) eats hard nuts and seeds, which it picks and cracks open with its tough, pointed bill. The bullfinch (center) feeds mainly on the buds of fruit trees, and its short, broad bill has a strong cutting action. The crossbill (bottom) reveals a specialized adaptation to a diet of conifer seeds. Its strange crossed-over bill is used to extract the seeds from their slots in the fresh cones.

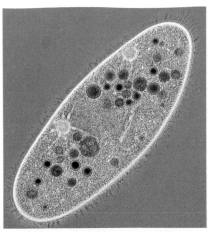

THE PRINCIPLE OF COMPETITIVE EXCLUSION

The Russian biologist G.F. Gause proposed that no two species can share the same niche. Rare exceptions have been found, but this is called Gause's principle. He demonstrated it experimentally with two species of a microscopic protozoan called paramecium (left). *Paramecium aurelia* has an advantage over *Paramecium caudatum*, as it can gain food more quickly. When the two species are grown together in laboratory conditions, *P. aurelia* increases in number and the *P. caudatum* population becomes extinct.

Kangaroo in Australia

Deer in the Northern Hemisphere

Long jaw

SIMILAR NICHES, SIMILAR ADAPTATIONS

Although they are unrelated and have very different bodies, there is a remarkable similarity between the faces of the deer and the kangaroo. This is because they are both adapted to the same niche, though on opposite sides of the globe. The niche that they occupy is that of a fast-moving planteater living in fairly open terrain. Their means of locomotion are quite different, the deer running on four long legs while the kangaroo leaps, using only its hindlimbs. However, both have long faces and a barrage of grinding teeth for dealing with tough vegetation.

A FLEXIBLE APPROACH TO SURVIVAL

Human activities can extend the niches for certain wild animals. The red fox is one of several species to benefit from the creation of towns and cities. Its niche is that of an opportunistic and generalized feeder, with good vision and a keen sense of smell. It has therefore been able to make use of the additional food supply and cover in built-up areas, moving undetected through alleyways and gardens, and scavenging on human refuse.

Notonecta water bug

Corixa water bug

Giant panda

A SPECIALIZATION TOO FAR

The giant panda exploits a niche that no other species can, by feeding almost entirely on bamboo shoots, although its ancestors were meat eaters. The price that a species pays for being so specialized is that it is vulnerable to changes in the environment. Most of the bamboo forests in the panda's native China have been destroyed. When much of the remaining bamboo flowered and died back in the early 1980s, part of a natural 100-year cycle, the giant panda was brought close to extinction.

NO COMPETITION

These two species of water bug are often found together in ponds. They look very much like each other and have many similar adaptations to the habitat that they share. However, there is no direct competition between the two species, because they occupy totally separate niches. In fact they feed at different trophic levels (p. 10). Notonecta is an active predator, a secondary consumer, eating other invertebrates, tadpoles, and even small fish. Corixa, by contrast, is a decomposer (p. 14), feeding on algae and rotting vegetation. The two water bugs can therefore survive side by side because they exploit completely different resources in the environment.

Studying populations

THE WAYS IN WHICH populations of particular species expand and decrease, and the reasons for these changes in numbers, form the subject matter of population dynamics. A close examination of the ways in which populations fluctuate reveals that, even in what may seem a very stable natural system, there are dynamic forces that can have dramatic effects and produce wild swings in numbers. Lemmings provide a vivid example. These small rodents inhabit the cold northern regions of the Northern Hemisphere. Every three to four years the lemmings become extremely abundant, and then they can be seen migrating in large numbers. It is thought that this occurs when they outstrip their food supplies. Tales of lemmings committing suicide are based on the fact that they will swim across rivers in search of food. When they reach the sea, they attempt to cross that too, and drown as a result.

White feathers for winter camouflage

PREDATOR AND PREY

The snowy owl, seen here swooping down on a vole, lives mainly in the tundra of North America and Eurasia, where it is normally a rare sight. However, every three or four years, snowy owls suddenly appear in large numbers and invade towns across the US, even as far south as Georgia. This strange phenomenon appears to be linked to the cyclical population changes of the lemming, on which the snowy owl feeds. As the lemmings reach plague proportions, the snowy owls, provided with a plentiful food supply, increase rapidly in numbers. When the lemmings migrate and their numbers dwindle, the owls too must migrate in search of food. They disperse over a wide area and their numbers then drop to low levels for the next two years. Such cyclical fluctuations are observed most commonly in the least complex ecosystems, such as the tundra of the Northern Hemisphere. This may be because these areas have relatively few species (low biodiversity) and are therefore naturally more unstable.

Powerful claw with long talons for gripping

Thick fur for warmth

Lichen-covered rock

CYCLICAL CHANGE

Several species are subject to cycles of rising and falling population numbers, though many questions about this behavior remain unanswered. Voles in northern latitudes (left) have a similar cycle to the lemming, possibly based on a cycle of plant growth. One explanation may be that as the size of the population increases, so more and more of the vital nutrients in the environment become locked up in the form of droppings. In the cold Arctic conditions, where decomposition takes a long time, these nutrients are released very slowly. Plant growth suffers, and the vegetation can only begin to recover after the rodents have migrated. As plant growth improves, the rodents return, and the cycle begins again.

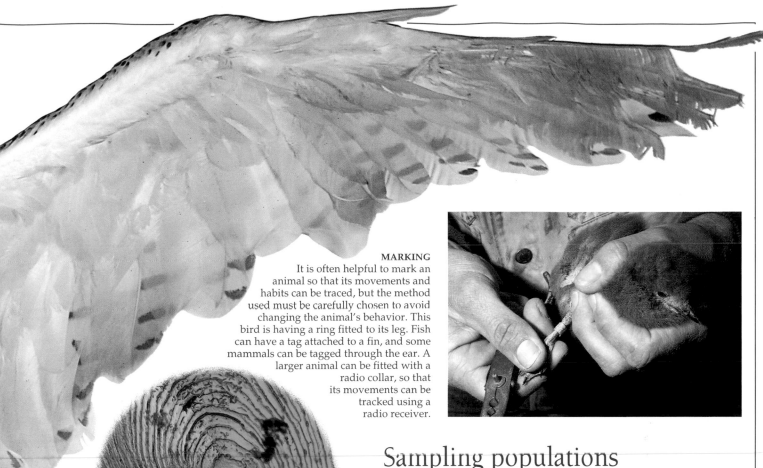

MARKING

It is often helpful to mark an animal so that its movements and habits can be traced, but the method used must be carefully chosen to avoid changing the animal's behavior. This bird is having a ring fitted to its leg. Fish can have a tag attached to a fin, and some mammals can be tagged through the ear. A larger animal can be fitted with a radio collar, so that its movements can be tracked using a radio receiver.

GROWTH RINGS

An animal's age can be worked out in a variety of ways – for example, by looking at the wear on a mammal's teeth. In the case of fish, the scales provide a useful indication of age, because they reveal dark rings (magnified above) that are formed each year during the winter, when growth is slowest. Ecologists can use this method to determine the age structure of a fish population, calculate how it will change over time, and decide how many fish can safely be caught in subsequent years without placing the population at risk.

Sampling populations

An understanding of how populations of fish, pests, crops, or rare animals behave has practical benefits for food production and for conservation. Population studies require information about the number of individuals in a population and the number found in a given area (the population density), the changes in population over time, the birth rate, and the death rate. Because it is impossible to collect an entire population, this information must be gained by capturing a few members and estimating the figures from this sample. Such samples are the basis for much of our scientific understanding of populations.

TRAPPING

Nets are used to catch birds and fish for study, but mammals such as this Australian bandicoot must be attracted to elaborate traps if they are to be released unharmed. The appropriate food is usually placed in the trap to act as a bait.

BOOMING AND BUSTING

Gathering long-term data about populations can take many years, but the ecologist Charles Elton (p. 30) was able to use historical records from the Hudson's Bay Company to produce this population graph of two species in the Canadian Arctic. It shows that every nine or ten years the number of snowshoe hares rises to a peak and then drops dramatically. The lynx population follows closely behind that of the snowshoe hare, on which the lynx depends for food. This "boom and bust" cycle, which is still not fully understood, is characteristic of several animal species living in extreme environmental conditions, such as the tundra or the desert.

Snowshoe hare

Lynx

Checks on population growth

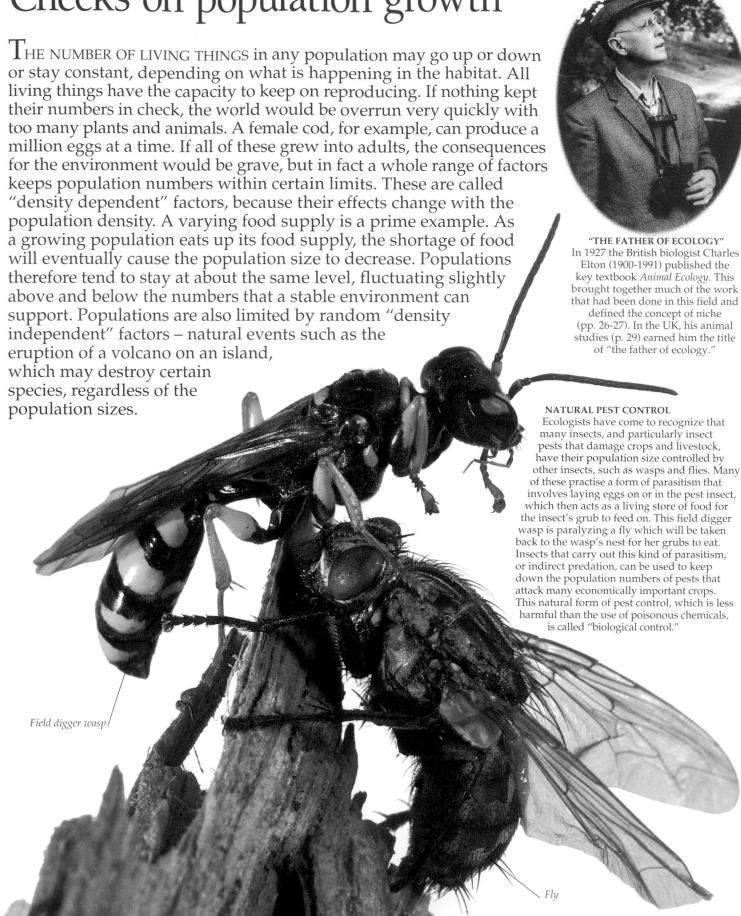

THE NUMBER OF LIVING THINGS in any population may go up or down or stay constant, depending on what is happening in the habitat. All living things have the capacity to keep on reproducing. If nothing kept their numbers in check, the world would be overrun very quickly with too many plants and animals. A female cod, for example, can produce a million eggs at a time. If all of these grew into adults, the consequences for the environment would be grave, but in fact a whole range of factors keeps population numbers within certain limits. These are called "density dependent" factors, because their effects change with the population density. A varying food supply is a prime example. As a growing population eats up its food supply, the shortage of food will eventually cause the population size to decrease. Populations therefore tend to stay at about the same level, fluctuating slightly above and below the numbers that a stable environment can support. Populations are also limited by random "density independent" factors – natural events such as the eruption of a volcano on an island, which may destroy certain species, regardless of the population sizes.

"THE FATHER OF ECOLOGY"
In 1927 the British biologist Charles Elton (1900-1991) published the key textbook *Animal Ecology*. This brought together much of the work that had been done in this field and defined the concept of niche (pp. 26-27). In the UK, his animal studies (p. 29) earned him the title of "the father of ecology."

NATURAL PEST CONTROL
Ecologists have come to recognize that many insects, and particularly insect pests that damage crops and livestock, have their population size controlled by other insects, such as wasps and flies. Many of these practise a form of parasitism that involves laying eggs on or in the pest insect, which then acts as a living store of food for the insect's grub to feed on. This field digger wasp is paralyzing a fly which will be taken back to the wasp's nest for her grubs to eat. Insects that carry out this kind of parasitism, or indirect predation, can be used to keep down the population numbers of pests that attack many economically important crops. This natural form of pest control, which is less harmful than the use of poisonous chemicals, is called "biological control."

Field digger wasp

Fly

Reindeer

THE LIMITING FACTOR
In 1944 a small group of 27 reindeer was introduced on to St. Matthew Island, off the northwest coast of Alaska. In less than 20 years, the population had grown to 6,000. Following a hard winter at the end of 1963, the population then crashed to just 42 individuals. The lichen on the island, the deers' usual food, had almost disappeared and an examination of the dead deer revealed that they had starved to death. In the absence of any predators, the density-dependent factor that had so dramatically reduced the number of reindeer was clearly the food supply.

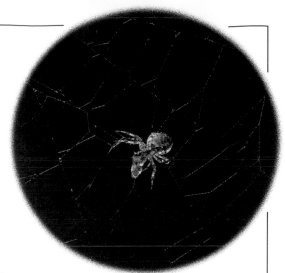

A DEVASTATING DISEASE
These tunnels in elm wood were made by the grubs of the elm bark beetle. In the early 1970s, a new strain of the fungus that causes Dutch elm disease was introduced into the UK on logs imported from Canada. The spores of the fungus were carried into British elm trees by the elm bark beetle. Within seven years, the fungus had wiped out nearly two-thirds of the elm trees in southern Britain. The British elms had evolved in the absence of this strain, and had no resistance to this form of population check.

THE IMPACT OF PREDATORS
Predation is one way in which populations are kept in check. Spiders are major predators of the insect population. It has been estimated that in temperate conditions, spiders can number almost 5 million per hectare (2 million per acre) at certain times of the year. Given that a spider eats at least 100 insects in a year, it can be calculated that in most temperate countries the annual weight of insects eaten by spiders is greater than the weight of the country's human population.

This gives some indication of the enormous impact that predators can have on a class of prey. When the relationship between predator and prey is long established and stable, predation can be beneficial to both parties, preventing the prey population from exceeding the limits that other factors in the environment, such as food supply, would impose.

THREATS TO LIFE
This table shows the different factors responsible for reducing the 200 eggs laid by a female winter moth to just two that survive to complete their life cycle, become adults, and breed. The survival of the brood depends on the time at which the eggs hatch, which must coincide with the opening of the oak buds on which the young caterpillars feed. If the eggs hatch too early, before the buds of the oak are open, or too late, when the leaves are too tough to eat, the caterpillars die. This accounts for the high number of "winter disappearances" of caterpillars.

NUMBER OF EGGS LAID BY A FEMALE WINTER MOTH	200
Cause of death	**Number killed**
Winter disappearance (death of some eggs and high mortality of newly hatched caterpillars)	184
Parasitic fly living on caterpillars	1
Other parasites living on caterpillars	1.5
Disease of caterpillars	2.5
Predators (shrews and beetles) killing pupae in soil	8.5
Parasitic wasp living on pupae	0.5
Total	198
NUMBER OF ADULTS SURVIVING TO BREED	2

Male robin

PROCLAIMING A TERRITORY
Members of the same species inevitably share a niche, and they therefore compete for resources, such as food, space, and breeding partners. Some species limit the number of individuals in an area by claiming and maintaining territories – each individual defends a geographical space, especially during the breeding season when extra food must be found for growing youngsters. The male robin's song and brightly colored breast warn off other males from entering his territory, and he will fight off intruders. Individuals that cannot find a territory will fail to attract a mate and will not breed. In this way, competition within the species is controlled.

LAYING THE SEEDS OF A PLAGUE
Unlike Arctic animals that have regular cycles (p. 28), some species of insects are subject to irregular population explosions. Desert locusts, for example, reach plague proportions when there is high rainfall. The rain provides the moist conditions needed to stimulate the development of locust eggs that have been laid in the sand. The rain also encourages the growth of the plants on which the locusts feed. Without the checks that large numbers of predators or parasites would provide, the locusts form gigantic swarms and consume all the vegetation in the region, including crops, causing famine in some areas. This is an example of the effect of a density independent factor, and ecologists study weather conditions in order to predict years of high rainfall, so that they can control locust plagues.

Locust laying eggs in sand

Family strategies

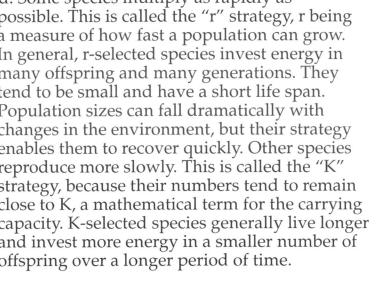

IN ANY ENVIRONMENT there is a limit to the resources available for any particular species. This is known by ecologists as the carrying capacity. In other words, there is only so much food or space available to support a population. Different organisms respond in different ways to their environment, and there are two principal survival strategies by which plants and animals exploit the available resources in order for the species to succeed. Some species multiply as rapidly as possible. This is called the "r" strategy, r being a measure of how fast a population can grow. In general, r-selected species invest energy in many offspring and many generations. They tend to be small and have a short life span. Population sizes can fall dramatically with changes in the environment, but their strategy enables them to recover quickly. Other species reproduce more slowly. This is called the "K" strategy, because their numbers tend to remain close to K, a mathematical term for the carrying capacity. K-selected species generally live longer and invest more energy in a smaller number of offspring over a longer period of time.

SLOW AND STEADY
In large mammals that follow the K strategy, the young are described as "precocial" – they are born in an advanced state of maturity. The elephant, for example, has a long pregnancy, one calf is born at a time, and considerable energy and time are invested in nurturing the young. In this way the strategy helps ensure that the young survive to breed.

ALLEE'S PRINCIPLE
In his book *Animal Aggregations*, the American zoologist Warder Clyde Allee (1885-1955) noted that in some animal species individuals group together for a variety of beneficial reasons. His view of animal behavior, emphasizing cooperation rather than competition, had a profound influence on ecological theory.

Blue and yellow macaw – a K-selected species

DIFFERENT STRATEGIES
Two related species of bird, the budgerigar of the arid regions of Australia and the blue and yellow macaw of the tropical forests of South America, show very different survival strategies. The budgerigar is an opportunistic species or "r strategist," laying many eggs and having a short life span. The blue and yellow macaw is an equilibrium species or "K strategist," producing fewer eggs and living for a long time. Much of this difference in strategy is due to the different habitats of the two species. In order to deal with the dry and difficult conditions of the Australian outback, the budgerigar must be able to profit from the abundant resources when the rains come. It does this by quickly producing large numbers of young. In the stable conditions of the tropical forest, the macaw can invest more time in its offspring.

Nest of baby mice

MANY AND OFTEN
Small mammals tend to be r strategists. The main difference between them and the K strategists can be seen in the number of young that they bear and the frequency with which they do so. The young, which can number up to 10 in the case of some mice, are described as "altricial," This means that they are born at a very immature stage of development, allowing the mother to become pregnant again and produce another brood while the conditions in the environment are right.

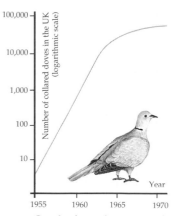

Graph of population size of collared dove over time

EXPLOITING A NICHE
In a period of just 25 years from its first arrival in the UK, the collared dove became a common sight. This rapid increase, growing by a factor of 10 every 2.3 years, shows that the dove was able to exploit a previously unoccupied niche (pp. 26-27). The flattening out of the top of the growth curve reveals that the size of the collared dove population stabilized without exceeding the carrying capacity.

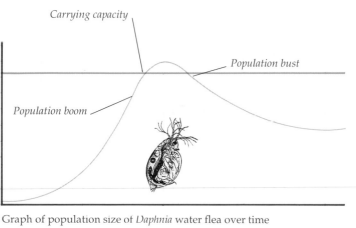

Graph of population size of *Daphnia* water flea over time

DAPHNIA WATER FLEA
This graph shows the changing size of a population of *Daphnia* water fleas being grown in the laboratory. The curve is described as "J-shaped," and it is typical of the population growth of an extremely r-selected species under favourable conditions. The population of animals increases rapidly and then falls away as the numbers exceed the carrying capacity of the environment. When observed under natural conditions, this curve indicates a "boom or bust" species such as the snowshoe hare (p. 29).

Yeast culture at time 1

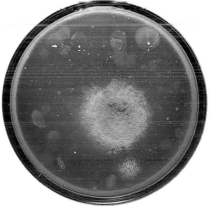

Yeast culture at time 2

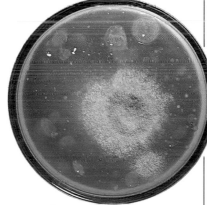

Yeast culture at time 3

Australian budgerigar – an r-selected species

GROWING WITHIN LIMITS
This graph shows the changing size of a population of yeast fungus being grown under laboratory conditions. The curve is described as S-shaped, and it is the typical growth curve for most organisms. From a gradual start, the population size rises fairly rapidly, slows down, and then levels out as the population approaches the carrying capacity. As the colony grows, the individuals reduce their reproduction rate in response to such factors as food exhaustion and the buildup of waste material. The effects of these increase as the population increases, so they are density dependent factors (p. 30). The example of the collared dove (top) shows how a species responds to similar factors in the wild.

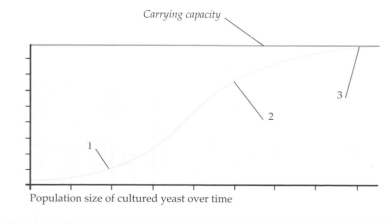

Population size of cultured yeast over time

Time and nature

ALTHOUGH A LAWN APPEARS to be a stable environment, only careful cutting and regular maintenance prevent it from changing. Left to its own devices, the lawn fills with weeds. Taller plants grow up and choke the grass, and it quickly becomes scrubland. In any temperate part of the world, the lawn would then go on to become a forest. Then it would cease to change, as the forest is the "climax vegetation." This process of transformation, as one kind of community succeeds another, is known as ecological succession, and it involves various kinds of changes. Different species succeed each other, so species that appear early in the process are unlikely to play an important role later on. The diversity of species increases, so that at climax there are more niches to be exploited. The total amount of organic matter present increases, as does the amount of energy being used, but the rate of production slows down, so that in a mature forest the rate of tree growth will have passed its peak.

STUDYING SUCCESSION
Frederic E. Clements (1874-1926), an American ecologist, pioneered the use of the quadrat (p. 24) to study and identify the different species that make up a community. His initial work was carried out in the grasslands of Nebraska. By clearing a measured area of all its vegetation, he showed that in each geographical zone, plants succeed each other in a particular sequence, developing toward a "climax" vegetation specific to that zone.

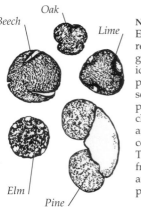

Beech *Oak* *Lime* *Elm* *Pine*

NATURAL HISTORY
Every species of plant requires particular growing conditions. The identities of microscopic pollen grains in deep soil samples therefore provide ecologists with clues about the climate and other environmental conditions in the past. These pollen grains are ' from five species of tree, and they can be positively identified.

ECOLOGICAL HISTORY WRITTEN ON THE LANDSCAPE
This coastal scene shows an environment undergoing both dramatic change and the more gradual process of succession. The sea is eroding the land, and the roots of a large tree have been undermined, causing it to fall. The sea has also deposited sand to form a long spit that stretches away into the distance. The spit has prevented water draining away from the land, forming a lagoon. The banks of the lagoon display a sequence of different phases of succession. A large reed bed marks the beginning of the process that will eventually turn the area of water into land, because the reeds accumulate particles of silt and clay. As the reeds grow forward, the land behind them becomes drier and suitable for sedges and grasses. These provide a foothold for alder trees, which thrive in moist soil. The alders in turn give way to larger tree species that need drier ground, such as oak.

Fallen tree

Soil eroded by action of sea

Sand bar deposited by the sea

MAINTAINING THE STATUS QUO

In nature, the change to a climax is often held back by a range of natural factors. Climatic conditions, such as frequent severe winds or very low temperatures, may prevent a community from reaching the climax state. In some cases, periodical fires will cause an environment to remain the same. Biological agents play an important role, too. Some grasslands owe their continued existence in that form to the grazing of the animals, such as rabbits, that live on them. By keeping the grass short and eating new shoots, these animals prevent new and different plants from becoming established.

FROM BARE ATOLL TO ISLAND PARADISE

Like any other bare surface, an exposed coral reef (pp. 46-47) is an inhospitable environment for most living things. However, over time, the reef's limestone is weathered by wind, rain, and sea. This weathering breaks the surface into particles that combine with other material and become trapped in cracks and crevices. Seeds that land in these pockets of nutrients will germinate and grow into plants, starting the first stages of succession. Eventually, the organic material from dead plants builds up with the other particles to form soil deep enough to support a widening range of plants and turn the coral island green.

DESTRUCTION AND REGENERATION

The eruption of a volcano can have a highly destructive effect on the surrounding landscape by covering large areas in a hot blanket of molten lava and fallen ash. Nonetheless, the process of succession is soon under way, and it is not long before recolonization begins. Once the land has cooled, any seeds brought by the wind or carried on the bodies of animals can profit from the nutrient-rich ash, as long as there is sufficient moisture. Even the area around the volcano of Krakatoa, which exploded with devastating violence in 1883, was quickly recolonized.

Reed beds

Alder and oak trees

Lagoon

Oak trees

Erosion of footpath

Reed beds

Sedges and grasses

Ferns

Alder tree

Ecology and evolution

ECOLOGY IS THE STUDY of the ways in which organisms interact with each other and with all the elements in the environment. When observing animals or plants, it is also important to take into account the history of the environment and the evolution of the ancestors of all the species alive today. The interaction between organisms and their environment has been going on since life itself began some 3,500 million years ago. In fact, it is thought that early living things (bacteria that began to capture the energy from sunlight) released the oxygen that made the evolution of other life forms possible. The presence of oxygen also led to the creation of the ozone layer that protects life from the Sun's lethal ultraviolet radiation. The environment helped create life and life helped create the environment for further life. When looked at in this way, the study of evolution – how particular organisms have adapted to particular niches and have in turn influenced the environment – can be seen as the study of ecology over a longer time scale.

ECOSYSTEMS APPROACH
The British botanist Arthur Tansley (1871-1955) was a pioneer in the study of plant communities, using sampling methods similar to those developed by Frederic Clements (p. 34). He was an advocate of an ecological approach to botany, and his work contributed to the formation of the British Ecological Society in 1913, the first such society in the world. Tansley felt strongly that ecological studies show how unwise it is to exploit the environment, and he became a leading figure in the conservation movement. It was Tansley who, in 1935, coined the word "ecosystem."

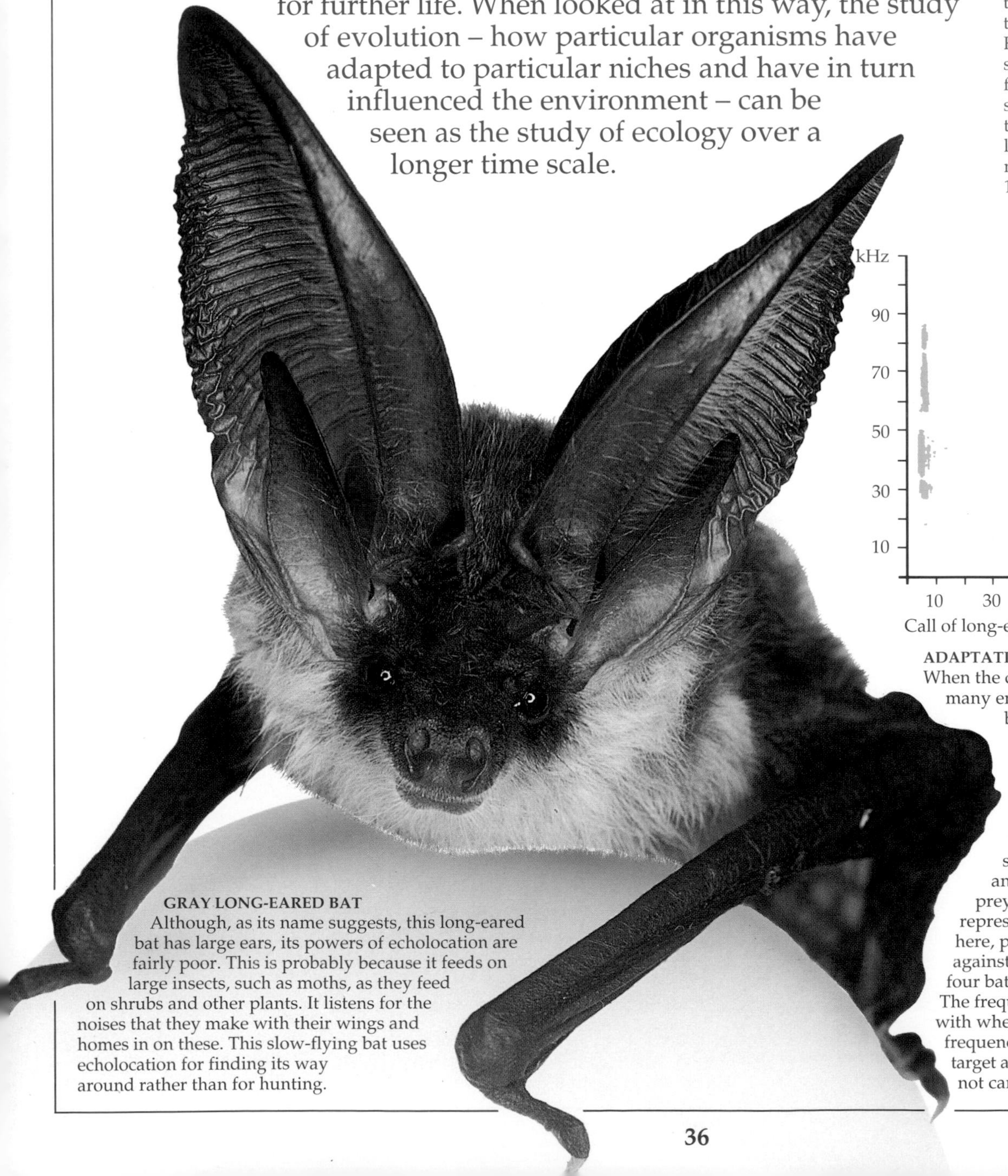

Call of long-eared bat

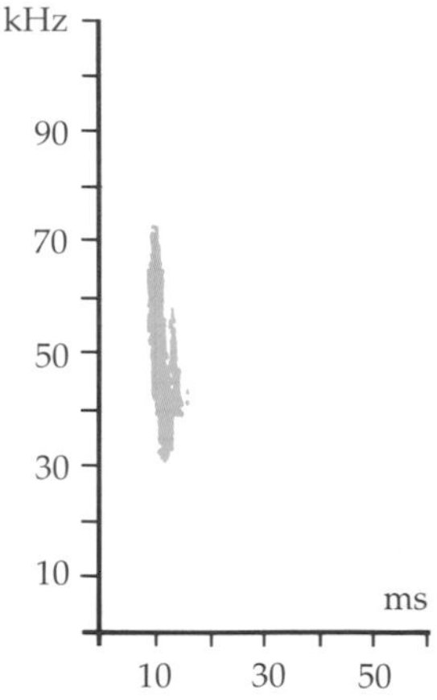

Call of whiskered bat

GRAY LONG-EARED BAT
Although, as its name suggests, this long-eared bat has large ears, its powers of echolocation are fairly poor. This is probably because it feeds on large insects, such as moths, as they feed on shrubs and other plants. It listens for the noises that they make with their wings and homes in on these. This slow-flying bat uses echolocation for finding its way around rather than for hunting.

ADAPTATION AND DIVERSITY
When the dinosaurs and other groups died out, many empty niches were left to be exploited by those organisms that had survived. In the air at night, bats found huge, rich, and almost unexploited niches, to which they rapidly adapted. They have divided up their habitat by evolving in different ways, as these small graphs, or sonograms, show. Bats send out beams of sound and use the reflected sound to locate prey and objects. Each sonogram represents the call of one of the bats shown here, plotting frequency (in kilohertz) against time (in milliseconds). Although all four bats eat insects, their calls differ widely. The frequencies that they use can be linked with where and how they hunt. High frequencies are good for pinpointing a nearby target and for locating obstacles, but they do not carry as far as lower frequency sounds.

NATHUSIUS' PIPISTRELLE BAT
Using fairly low frequencies at the end of its call (below left), Nathusius' pipistrelle hunts in open terrain, locating small flying insects at considerable distances.

In any population there is considerable natural variation, and it is on this variation that natural selection acts to produce evolution. In the case of the grass called Yorkshire fog, certain individuals happen to be able to tolerate unnaturally high concentrations of copper in the soil. Normally these plants have no advantage and their numbers in the population remain insignificantly small. However, on soil contaminated with waste from copper mines, the individuals that have this tolerance are able to survive, and eventually the population consists only of those that can tolerate high copper levels in the soil. The initial natural variation within the species has enabled it to adapt to this peculiar environmental niche.

Call of Nathusius' pipistrelle bat

Call of noctule bat

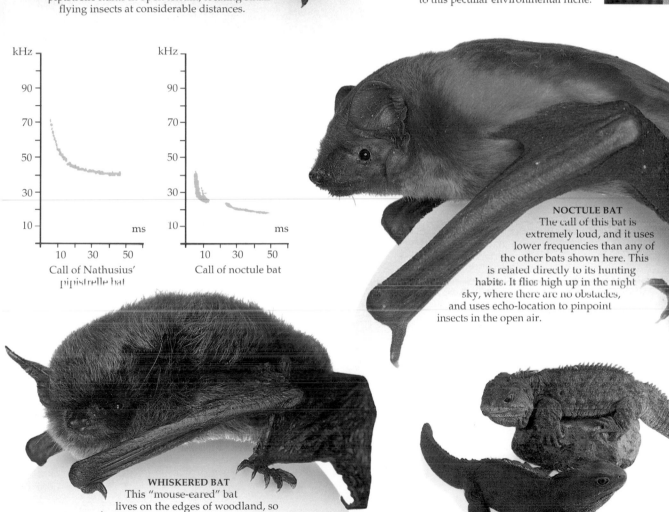

NOCTULE BAT
The call of this bat is extremely loud, and it uses lower frequencies than any of the other bats shown here. This is related directly to its hunting habits. It flies high up in the night sky, where there are no obstacles, and uses echo-location to pinpoint insects in the open air.

WHISKERED BAT
This "mouse-eared" bat lives on the edges of woodland, so its need to avoid obstacles is less than that of the long-eared bat. It uses slightly lower frequencies and uses its call to locate small insects in the air.

THE RISE OF THE SUPER RAT
Adaptability can make pest control difficult. Rats, which damage food stores and spread disease, have been controlled with a poison called Warfarin. Initially this proved very effective, but some rats had a degree of resistance to the poison and survived. Their offspring inherited this resistance and gradually Warfarin ceased to kill them. Each time the poison is improved, natural resistance in some rats has allowed the population to bounce back, producing the highly resistant "super rat". This adaptability has made it hard to reduce the world rat population.

LIVING FOSSILS
These tuatara, found on isolated islands off the coast of New Zealand, are the sole remaining members of a group that died out many millions of years ago. These reptiles have survived relatively unchanged since the time of the dinosaurs. Changes in climate and other environmental factors seem to have had little impact on them, and there has been little pressure on them to evolve. Such animals can truly be called living fossils. Crocodiles are another example of creatures that have survived almost unchanged. The dinosaurs were an outstandingly successful and very diverse group, and they dominated all other life on Earth for many millions of years. However, when the environment changed, possibly due to the impact of a meteor some 65 million years ago, they were unable to adapt to the new situation and they gradually died out.

Life in the ocean

ALTHOUGH THE WORLD'S OCEANS appear to contain little plant life (apart from seaweed around the shores), sunlight and photosynthesis are the major source of energy for life in the oceans, as they are in all ecosystems. It is just that the phytoplankton – the plants at the base of the ocean food web – are not readily visible. Because sunlight can only penetrate a short distance into the waters, only the surface layers can support the generation of new plant life. These plants also need nutrients, and these are unevenly distributed throughout the oceans, being carried by the ocean currents that move the waters around the planet. Since these factors, as well as temperature and salinity, affect the productivity of plant life, some parts of the oceans are very rich in phytoplankton and other forms of life in the food chain, while some areas are virtually lifeless.

POISONOUS PIRATE
The infamous Portuguese man-of-war has a "sail" that allows it to be blown effortlessly through the water. It comes across its prey by chance and paralyzes it with long, deadly, stinging tentacles.

Sail

Whiplike tail

Venomous spine

INVISIBLE LINKS IN THE CHAIN OF LIFE
Where the ocean is richly supplied with light and nutrients, the microscopic world of plankton forms the base of the food chain. Phytoplankton consists of tiny plants, such as diatoms and algae, with short life spans and a rapid turnover of population. They are eaten by zooplankton (magnified right), tiny animals that drift in the ocean currents. These include small crustaceans and the larvae of far larger animals, such as fish, crabs, and jellyfish. These are eaten by bigger zooplankton, and by a range of filter feeders from mollusks up to the largest of all animals, the blue whale.

UP THE CHAIN
Young cod feed at the surface on small crustaceans, but as they grow they change their diet, feeding farther up the food chain (p. 10). They move down to deeper water and take crustaceans, small fish, and worms. When larger, they feed almost entirely on other fish. Food chains in the ocean are often much longer than those on land, because several fish in the chain may be carnivorous, feeding on other fish and becoming the prey of yet larger fish.

Well-developed eye

Tentacle

A baby squid escapes in a flurry of ink

MOLLUSK WITH A DIFFERENCE
As both a predator and the potential prey of others, the squid is perfectly adapted to its ocean home. Although it is a mollusk, a member of the same group as the snail, it is totally unlike its land-dwelling cousin, having eyes like those of a vertebrate that enable it to watch out for food and for enemies. It moves through the water by jet propulsion and can camouflage itself rapidly, sending waves of color down its body to disguise its outline from enemies in open water. If a predator comes too close, it squirts a cloud of dark ink, to cover its escape.

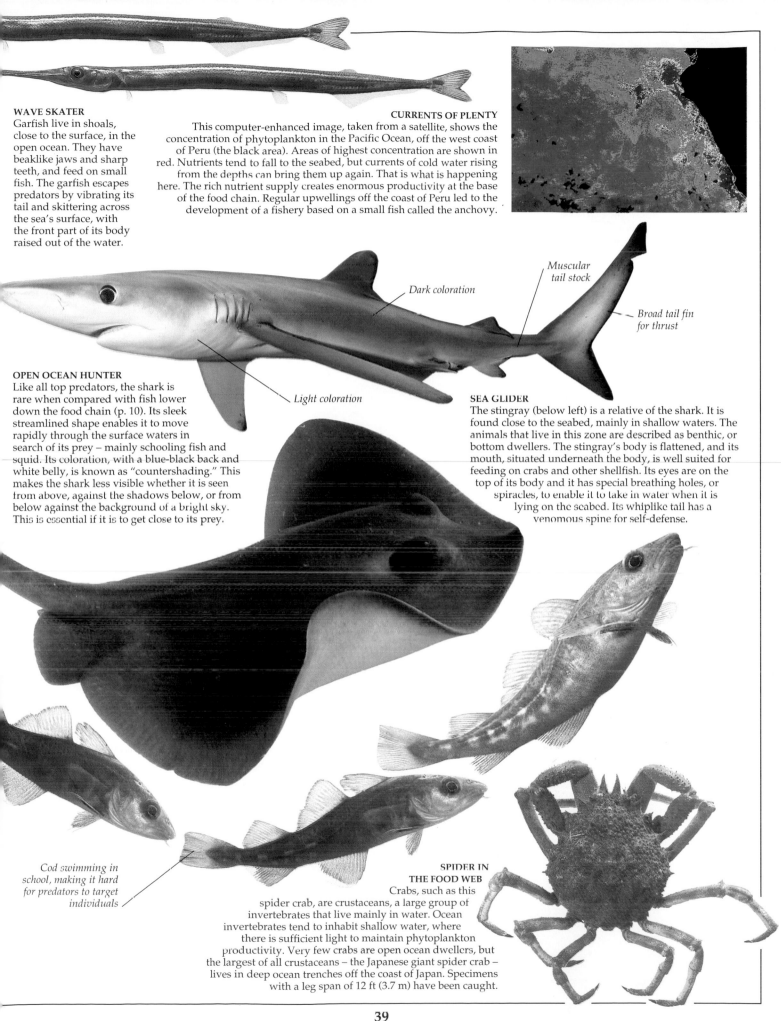

WAVE SKATER

Garfish live in shoals, close to the surface, in the open ocean. They have beaklike jaws and sharp teeth, and feed on small fish. The garfish escapes predators by vibrating its tail and skittering across the sea's surface, with the front part of its body raised out of the water.

CURRENTS OF PLENTY

This computer-enhanced image, taken from a satellite, shows the concentration of phytoplankton in the Pacific Ocean, off the west coast of Peru (the black area). Areas of highest concentration are shown in red. Nutrients tend to fall to the seabed, but currents of cold water rising from the depths can bring them up again. That is what is happening here. The rich nutrient supply creates enormous productivity at the base of the food chain. Regular upwellings off the coast of Peru led to the development of a fishery based on a small fish called the anchovy.

Muscular tail stock

Dark coloration

Broad tail fin for thrust

OPEN OCEAN HUNTER

Like all top predators, the shark is rare when compared with fish lower down the food chain (p. 10). Its sleek streamlined shape enables it to move rapidly through the surface waters in search of its prey – mainly schooling fish and squid. Its coloration, with a blue-black back and white belly, is known as "countershading." This makes the shark less visible whether it is seen from above, against the shadows below, or from below against the background of a bright sky. This is essential if it is to get close to its prey.

Light coloration

SEA GLIDER

The stingray (below left) is a relative of the shark. It is found close to the seabed, mainly in shallow waters. The animals that live in this zone are described as benthic, or bottom dwellers. The stingray's body is flattened, and its mouth, situated underneath the body, is well suited for feeding on crabs and other shellfish. Its eyes are on the top of its body and it has special breathing holes, or spiracles, to enable it to take in water when it is lying on the seabed. Its whiplike tail has a venomous spine for self-defense.

Cod swimming in school, making it hard for predators to target individuals

SPIDER IN THE FOOD WEB

Crabs, such as this spider crab, are crustaceans, a large group of invertebrates that live mainly in water. Ocean invertebrates tend to inhabit shallow water, where there is sufficient light to maintain phytoplankton productivity. Very few crabs are open ocean dwellers, but the largest of all crustaceans – the Japanese giant spider crab – lives in deep ocean trenches off the coast of Japan. Specimens with a leg span of 12 ft (3.7 m) have been caught.

Surviving in arid lands

THE FEATURES THAT CHARACTERIZE all deserts are lack of water – less than 10 in (25 cm) of rain per year – and generally harsh conditions. Desert conditions are found in many parts of the world (p. 9). The examples on this page are mainly from the US. Most deserts receive some rain, though it is highly unpredictable, and it is this potential source of water that makes life possible in this arid environment. Temperatures fluctuate widely, too. Many deserts are very hot in the day, but they can be extremely cold at night. Nutrients are limited compared with most other ecosystems, because there is too little moisture for bacteria and fungi that cause decomposition. However, a range of organisms has adapted to living with a slight and irregular supply of water and to conserving precious energy, so most deserts do support some life. Obtaining nutrients is a problem for all desert organisms, and it is thought that most of the plant biomass (p. 10) in deserts exists in the form of underground storage organs, such as roots and tubers.

THE EVER-GROWING DESERT
In areas of low rainfall, poor land management can rapidly lead to the desertification of once productive land, especially on the edges of existing desert. Around the Sahara desert in Africa, a growing population and a shortage of pasture have forced many people to move their livestock on to land that cannot withstand this extra pressure. As a result, large areas have become desert.

THE DESERT IN BLOOM
Desert plants are able to respond rapidly when sufficient rain eventually falls. In some cases, seeds can germinate, grow up into plants, and flower and produce seeds, all within two weeks. These short-lived flowers, called "ephemerals," often have brightly colored petals to attract the desert insects that are also going through a rapid life cycle. The seeds of some plants are coated with a chemical that prevents them from germinating until the rain washes the chemical away.

DEATH RATTLE IN THE ROCKS
The rattlesnake hunts its prey at night using heat-sensitive pits in its face. These can detect the presence of warmblooded prey like the kangaroo rat. The rattlesnake's bite injects a powerful venom that will kill the prey quickly, but not immediately. Using smell receptors in its tongue, the snake follows its dying victim and then devours it. This method of killing uses the minimum amount of energy, which is at a premium in the desert. This snake's unique rattle in the tail is thought to have evolved as a warning signal to keep away large animals that might trample on it. The rattlesnake, like all snakes, is deaf and is unable to hear its own sinister warning.

Camouflaged coloring with broken outline for rocky desert conditions

Heat-sensitive pit

Smell-sensitive tongue

Rattle

SAVING ENERGY WITH A STINGER IN THE TAIL
Like the rattlesnake, desert scorpions reduce the need for physical force in hunting by being extremely venomous, far more so than their relatives in other parts of the world. This enables them to deal with even quite large prey. The pincers of desert scorpions tend to be small, since a deadly sting reduces the need to wrestle with prey, which would use up precious energy.

Stinger

Small pincers

A THERMAL BALANCING ACT
Desert conditions favor reptiles: dry, scaly skin retains water, and a low metabolic rate enables them to last a long time without food. Small reptiles, like this collared lizard, can hide in rocks or in the sand to escape the sun and control their body temperature. Very fine control is needed because each reptile species has its own ideal operating temperature. For some desert lizards, this temperature is close to the point at which they would die.

Expandable ribs

Sharp bill to tear flesh

SPIKY WATER STORES
Cacti and other desert succulents have shallow, widespread root systems to absorb large amounts of rainwater very quickly. This can then be stored in the stems of the cacti, some of which are ribbed to permit expansion. Spines on the stem prevent animals from taking this stored water for their own use. Cacti have the unusual ability to take in carbon dioxide at night and store it in other chemical compounds. This means that the stomata (p. 9) are open to allow gas exchange when the air is cool, and this keeps water loss to a minimum. In daylight the stored carbon dioxide is released and used in photosynthesis.

EQUIPPED FOR THE KILL
The Harris' hawk is a top predator in the desert ecosystem of North America. Seeking a diet consisting mainly of reptiles, which may be thin on the ground, each individual needs a vast area as its hunting ground. An animal that eats reptiles must deal with a dinner that tends to be muscular and well equipped with teeth or fangs. The Harris' hawk has powerful talons to grip its squirming prey, and long legs with protective scales to keep its body out of harm's way.

Protective scales

Wide tail to control gliding

Powerful talons

Protective spines

DUNE DWELLER
All deserts have small rodents that, like this kangaroo rat, can survive without drinking. They obtain their moisture from the seeds they eat, and avoid wasting water by producing a very concentrated urine. They live in cool underground burrows, where relative humidity can be more than three times greater than it is above ground.

A world of ebb and flow

THE EDGE OF THE SEA is very different from the stable environment of the open ocean. Conditions on the shoreline are constantly changing with the daily rhythm of the tides. Some organisms are covered by the sea and then exposed to the air for many hours at a time. All must live with a changing depth of water, and with changes in temperature and salinity. The best-adapted are able to live high up the shore, exploiting a rich but difficult environment. The rocky shore provides a wealth of opportunity for many species. Its nooks and crannies are ideal for many species of mollusks, such as limpets, topshells, and winkles, which graze on the algae and seaweeds growing on the shore. These, in turn, are eaten by predators such as crabs, fish, and other mollusks. When the tide is out, many of these are to be found in rock pools, avoiding the drastic changes in temperature, salinity, and oxygen supply that exposure to the air can bring.

SEASHORE JUMBLE
A multitude of shells and seaweeds washed up on the shore shows the rich variety of life in the tidal zone.

FIRST LINKS IN THE SEASHORE FOOD CHAIN
Along with phytoplankton, algal organisms such as seaweeds are at the base of the food chain along the shoreline. They are adapted for life here in a variety of ways. Some have tough pliable fronds to cope with the battering of the waves. Some have a rootlike "holdfast" to secure them to the rocks. The bladderwrack has air-filled pockets to keep its fronds near the surface and catch as much light as possible. The paper-thin sea lettuce can tolerate a wide range of conditions, and is even found in polluted water. Red seaweed contains the pigment phycoerythrin, enabling it to live in murky water with little light. The seaweed-like sea mat, on which the starfish is lying, is in fact a colony of tiny filter-feeding animals called bryozoans. Each animal is protected by a case of chalky or horny material into which it can withdraw for protection.

SPINES AND STARS
Sea urchins cling to hard surfaces in great numbers, feeding on algae and small encrusting animals. The starfish, which is related to the sea urchin, is a major predator in the seashore community. It feeds by wrapping its "arms" around a shellfish, such as a mussel, and using its many gripping tube feet to pull the two halves of the shell apart. It then pushes its stomach out in between the shells and pours in digestive juices, creating a soup that it can absorb.

Bladderwrack seaweed

Starfish

Sea mat

Sea urchin

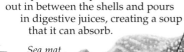

WIDE-RANGING FEEDERS
Shore crabs are found in all the zones of the shoreline, from the highest rock pool to water 20 ft (6 m) deep. They are voracious carnivores, feeding mainly on invertebrates, such as worms, but also scavenging decaying plant and animal matter, using their strong mouthparts to smash their food into smaller pieces. Shore crabs are therefore both secondary consumers (p. 10) and detritivores (p. 14).

Gold sinny

Cockle shells

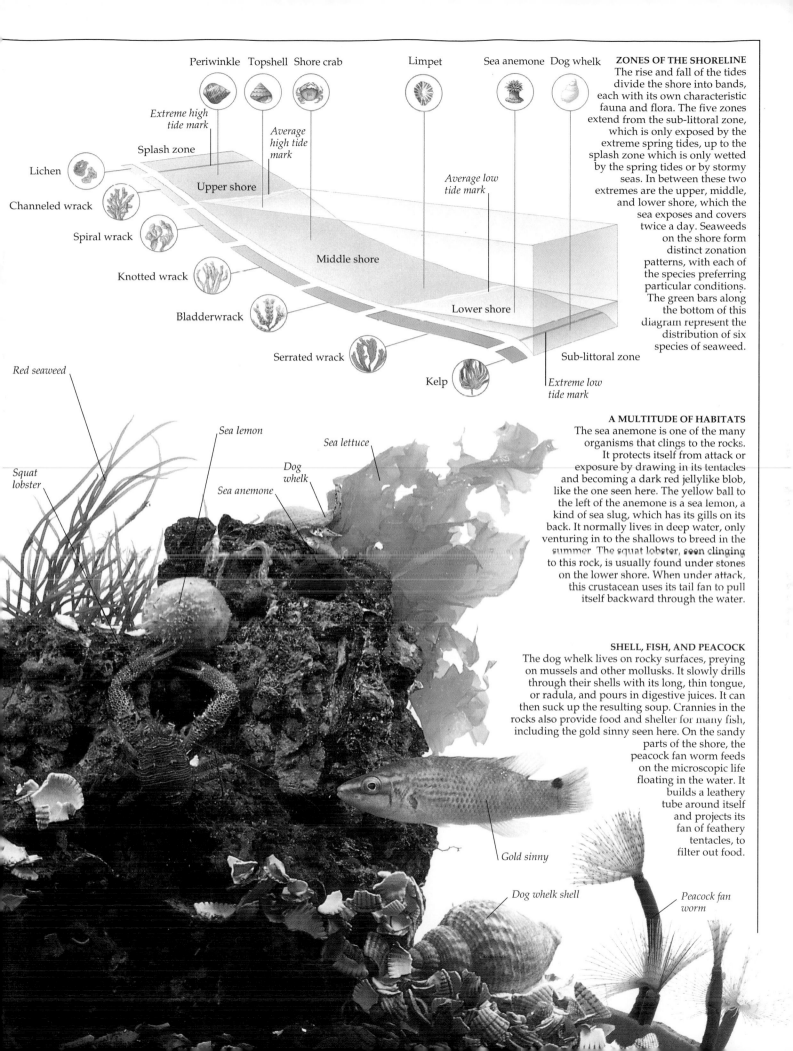

Periwinkle Topshell Shore crab

Limpet

Sea anemone Dog whelk

ZONES OF THE SHORELINE
The rise and fall of the tides
divide the shore into bands,
each with its own characteristic
fauna and flora. The five zones
extend from the sub-littoral zone,
which is only exposed by the
extreme spring tides, up to the
splash zone which is only wetted
by the spring tides or by stormy
seas. In between these two
extremes are the upper, middle,
and lower shore, which the
sea exposes and covers
twice a day. Seaweeds
on the shore form
distinct zonation
patterns, with each of
the species preferring
particular conditions.
The green bars along
the bottom of this
diagram represent the
distribution of six
species of seaweed.

Extreme high tide mark

Splash zone

Average high tide mark

Lichen

Upper shore

Average low tide mark

Channeled wrack

Spiral wrack

Knotted wrack

Middle shore

Bladderwrack

Lower shore

Serrated wrack

Sub-littoral zone

Kelp

Extreme low tide mark

Red seaweed

A MULTITUDE OF HABITATS
The sea anemone is one of the many
organisms that clings to the rocks.
It protects itself from attack or
exposure by drawing in its tentacles
and becoming a dark red jellylike blob,
like the one seen here. The yellow ball to
the left of the anemone is a sea lemon, a
kind of sea slug, which has its gills on its
back. It normally lives in deep water, only
venturing in to the shallows to breed in the
summer. The squat lobster, seen clinging
to this rock, is usually found under stones
on the lower shore. When under attack,
this crustacean uses its tail fan to pull
itself backward through the water.

Sea lemon

Sea lettuce

Dog whelk

Squat lobster

Sea anemone

SHELL, FISH, AND PEACOCK
The dog whelk lives on rocky surfaces, preying
on mussels and other mollusks. It slowly drills
through their shells with its long, thin tongue,
or radula, and pours in digestive juices. It can
then suck up the resulting soup. Crannies in the
rocks also provide food and shelter for many fish,
including the gold sinny seen here. On the sandy
parts of the shore, the
peacock fan worm feeds
on the microscopic life
floating in the water. It
builds a leathery
tube around itself
and projects its
fan of feathery
tentacles, to
filter out food.

Gold sinny

Dog whelk shell

Peacock fan worm

Leaves and needles

TWO MAIN KINDS OF FOREST grow in temperate regions (between the tropics and the polar circles). These are deciduous forests, containing mainly "hardwood" species such as beech, oak, hickory, and birch, and coniferous forests of "softwood" species like pine and fir. Before the spread of humans across the globe, much of the Northern Hemisphere was probably covered in forest, as this is the climax vegetation (p. 34) for this part of the world. In the last few centuries, large areas of European and North American forest have been cut down for use as fuel or building material, or to open up the land for agriculture. In many countries there is little untouched woodland left, and much of the coniferous forest has been artificially planted.

FOREST HUNTER
A predator at the top of the food chain in deciduous woodlands, the tawny owl feeds mainly on rodents and small birds, but it will eat frogs and even fish.

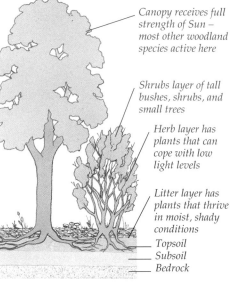

BROAD-LEAFED WOODLANDS
Deciduous trees have delicate flattened leaves to catch sunlight. They grow more slowly than conifers and do most of their growing in the spring. They lose their leaves in the autumn and regrow them the following spring.

Canopy receives full strength of Sun – most other woodland species active here

Shrubs layer of tall bushes, shrubs, and small trees

Herb layer has plants that can cope with low light levels

Litter layer has plants that thrive in moist, shady conditions
Topsoil
Subsoil
Bedrock

TREASURES OF THE FOREST FLOOR
The deciduous forest is rich and highly productive, producing up to 3 lb 5 oz (1.5 kg) of material (mainly wood) per square meter (10 sq ft) every year. The canopy produces a wide range of fruits, seeds, and berries, but because young plants cannot grow in the shadow of their parents, the seeds must be dispersed. Brightly colored berries attract birds that feed on them, and the seeds are then passed out in the droppings, away from the parent plant. Sycamore seeds have wings that allow the wind to carry them away as they fall. On the forest floor, mosses grow on rotting branches, and the annual fall of leaves – around 2,600 lb per acre – provides food for other organisms, such as the fungi and tiny animals that break all this down and recycle the nutrients.

DECIDUOUS LAYERS
Light levels decrease as one moves down from the canopy to the forest floor. The layering effect is rather similar to that found in the ocean.

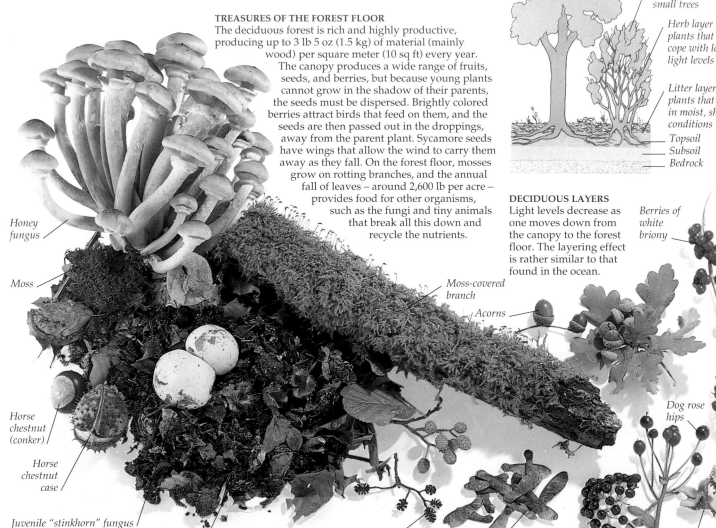

Honey fungus

Moss

Moss-covered branch

Acorns

Berries of white briony

Horse chestnut (conker)

Horse chestnut case

Dog rose hips

Juvenile "stinkhorn" fungus

Beechwood leaf litter

Alder cones

Sycamore seeds

Dogwood berries

Beechnut cases (beech mast)

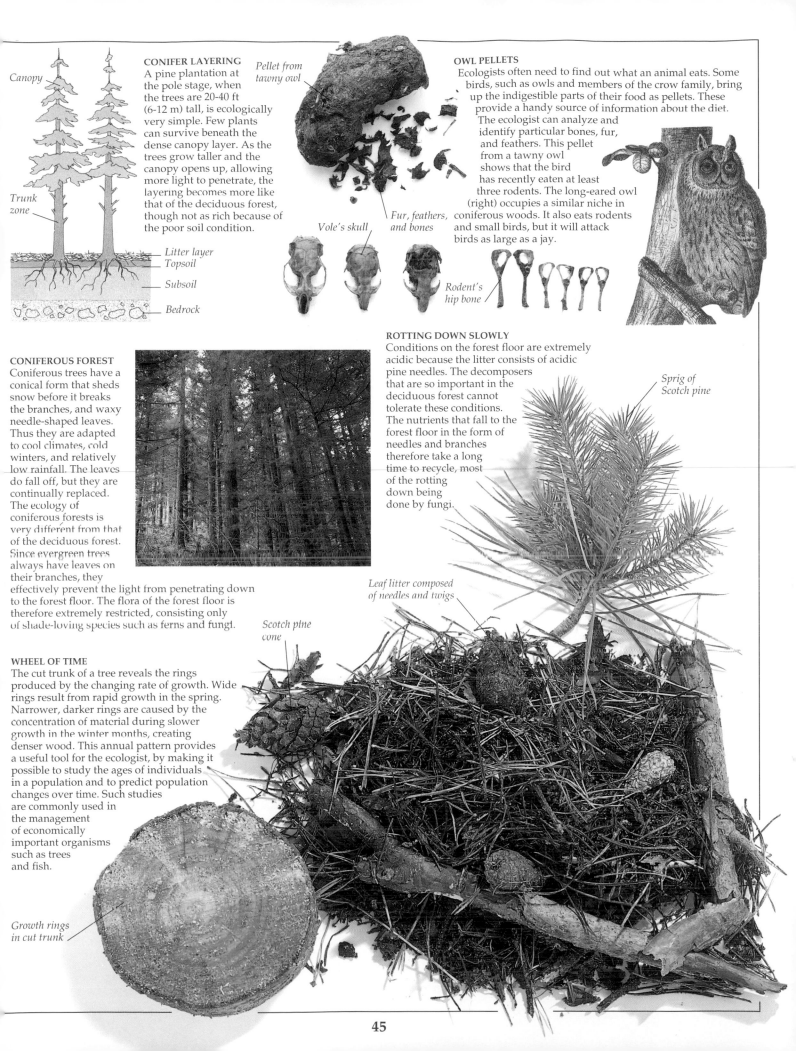

CONIFER LAYERING
A pine plantation at the pole stage, when the trees are 20-40 ft (6-12 m) tall, is ecologically very simple. Few plants can survive beneath the dense canopy layer. As the trees grow taller and the canopy opens up, allowing more light to penetrate, the layering becomes more like that of the deciduous forest, though not as rich because of the poor soil condition.

Canopy

Trunk zone

Pellet from tawny owl

Litter layer
Topsoil

Subsoil

Bedrock

Vole's skull

Fur, feathers, and bones

Rodent's hip bone

OWL PELLETS
Ecologists often need to find out what an animal eats. Some birds, such as owls and members of the crow family, bring up the indigestible parts of their food as pellets. These provide a handy source of information about the diet. The ecologist can analyze and identify particular bones, fur, and feathers. This pellet from a tawny owl shows that the bird has recently eaten at least three rodents. The long-eared owl (right) occupies a similar niche in coniferous woods. It also eats rodents and small birds, but it will attack birds as large as a jay.

CONIFEROUS FOREST
Coniferous trees have a conical form that sheds snow before it breaks the branches, and waxy needle-shaped leaves. Thus they are adapted to cool climates, cold winters, and relatively low rainfall. The leaves do fall off, but they are continually replaced. The ecology of coniferous forests is very different from that of the deciduous forest. Since evergreen trees always have leaves on their branches, they effectively prevent the light from penetrating down to the forest floor. The flora of the forest floor is therefore extremely restricted, consisting only of shade-loving species such as ferns and fungi.

ROTTING DOWN SLOWLY
Conditions on the forest floor are extremely acidic because the litter consists of acidic pine needles. The decomposers that are so important in the deciduous forest cannot tolerate these conditions. The nutrients that fall to the forest floor in the form of needles and branches therefore take a long time to recycle, most of the rotting down being done by fungi.

Sprig of Scotch pine

Leaf litter composed of needles and twigs

Scotch pine cone

WHEEL OF TIME
The cut trunk of a tree reveals the rings produced by the changing rate of growth. Wide rings result from rapid growth in the spring. Narrower, darker rings are caused by the concentration of material during slower growth in the winter months, creating denser wood. This annual pattern provides a useful tool for the ecologist, by making it possible to study the ages of individuals in a population and to predict population changes over time. Such studies are commonly used in the management of economically important organisms such as trees and fish.

Growth rings in cut trunk

45

Riches of the reef

CORAL POLYPS ARE SMALL MARINE ANIMALS that create limestone shells. These build up into massive structures called coral reefs, but only in waters that are warmer than 77 °F (25 °C) and less than 33 ft (10 m) deep. They are among the most productive ecosystems on Earth, achieving 3,000 times the photosynthetic productivity of the surrounding waters. The reef owes its wealth to a special relationship between corals and plants. Inside each polyp there are tens of thousands of single-celled plants called zooxanthellae, which supply the coral with additional energy through photosynthesis. They also recycle limited nutrients. Corals catch zooplankton and other prey, and the waste products are used by the zooxanthellae. The Odum brothers (p. 9) discovered this relationship when they calculated that the zooplankton in the surrounding sea could not provide enough energy and nutrients for the coral reef to survive. It was the zooxanthellae that provided the missing figures. Energy and nutrients are exchanged very efficiently in a coral reef and, as in the tropical rain forest, most of the nutrients are locked up in living organisms.

Powerful tail for thrust and steering

LOVELY LITTLE MOVER
Many reef-dwelling fish have enlarged fins, particularly the pectoral fins, so that they can scull delicately through the intricate maze of coral, and even go backward in small spaces. In the case of this mandarin fish, the broad pectoral fins are also brightly colored, possibly for signaling to other fish.

Large colorful pectoral fin

Distinctive blue band

Small tail

Deep flat body

Poisonous tentacles

MUTUAL BENEFIT
In nature, there are many examples of intimate associations between different species in which one or both of the organisms benefit. If one of the organisms harms the other in the process, the relationship is known as parasitism. If both benefit, the relationship is a mutualistic one. This clown fish is able to swim among the tentacles of the sea anemone without being stung, and in this way it is protected from the attention of predators. The sea anemone receives scraps of food that fall from the fish, so this is mutualism.

TALL, SLIM, AND COLORFUL
The blue-ringed angel fish is typical of those fish that live among the coral heads, having a deep slim body that allows it to glide through narrow slits. There is no need for a powerful tail, since it escapes from predators not through speed but by hiding in the reef's many crevices. In this colorful environment, many species make use of color for communication and species recognition, to attract potential mates, and to threaten one another over territorial disputes.

Dorsal fin

Streamlined body for speed

HUNTING ON THE MARGINS
The black tip reef shark can grow to a length of 8 ft (2.4 m) and is found around the edges of reefs. It does not have the slim body and maneuverability of fish that dwell in the coral reef. Instead, it is streamlined and is adapted for a deep-water life-style. This top predator patrols the waters near the reef, taking advantage of the high productivity by feeding on the fish that live there.

TOUGH LIPS FOR A TOUGH DIET
The trigger fish, with its deep body, is a typical reef dweller. It is able to maneuver its way through the corals to feed on hard-shelled invertebrates, including mollusks and spiny sea urchins. Its strong lips, with their protective horny covering, allow the trigger fish to bite the shells open. Some species of horny-lipped fish, such as the parrot fish, actually bite chunks of limestone off the coral reef and feed on the fleshy polyps living inside.

Pectoral fin

Strong jaws equipped with sharp teeth

Horny lips

LIMESTONE JUNGLE
The coral reef is a splendid patchwork of coral colonies, varying widely in shape and color. Being immobile, each species of coral breeds by releasing eggs and sperm into the water on the same night of the year to maximize the chances of fertilization. The newly formed polyps then drift in the currents until they land on a surface, usually the reef, and establish themselves.

PLAGUE OR CYCLE?
For years the Great Barrier Reef off the coast of northeastern Australia has been under attack from the "crown of thorns" starfish, which eats the living polyps and causes the coral skeleton to crumble. Although this reef stretches 1,250 miles (2,000 km) along the Queensland coast, there are fears that the sheer numbers of starfish could destroy the reef. Some scientists blame this plague on the fertilizers used to grow sugar cane. Run-off from the land may be entering the sea and providing nutrients that support the starfish larvae, but experiments do not support this theory. Others think it is a natural phenomenon that may benefit the reef by killing off old parts and allowing new species to move in. Twenty years of research have failed to provide an answer to this puzzle.

Spotted sweetlip

Cleaner wrasse

DENTAL HYGIENE
A cleaner wrasse picking parasites from the mouth of a spotted sweetlip provides a good example of cooperation in the coral reef system. Several species of "cleaner" fish and shrimps find food by eating parasites from the skin, mouth, and gills of large fish that would normally prey on them. On some reefs, fish have been observed gathering at "cleaning stations," waiting in line for their turn to be cleaned.

INSIDE THE CORAL POLYP
Like sea anemones, corals have tentacles for catching prey, which is passed down to the stomach. Corals also produce limestone cups. As successive generations of coral live and die, so these hard rocky shells build up to form solid reefs, which the corals continue to colonize.

Tentacles

Limestone cup

Stomach

Sharing the grasslands

THE SAVANNAH OF EAST AFRICA is among the best known of the world's grasslands. Despite two wet seasons each year, the unpredictable and sparse rainfall ensures that this area remains grassland all year round. Grass tolerates dry conditions and grasslands have much in common with desert and arid regions. Rich volcanic soils provide much of the nutrient supply for the grasses, which are the main source of food for the primary consumers – vast herds of antelope and other herbivores. These sustain several species of large carnivores – mainly lions, hyenas, and leopards. Grass is very adaptable and can survive being trampled, burned, chewed, and cut, because the leaves grow from just under the ground and will quickly regrow. Humans often burn grasslands in the belief that this will nourish the following year's growth, but not all ecologists agree. However, the combination of dry conditions, burning, and heavy grazing do ensure that grasslands stay unchanged.

SCAVENGER
Vultures live on the remains of dead animals, mainly from kills left by predators such as lions. As decomposers, they play a vital role in the grassland food chain. Each species eats a different part of the carcass. Roupell's griffon vulture can reach inside the body cavity.

SHARING LIMITED RESOURCES
The grassland habitat shows a limited diversity of plant species, but a large variety of herbivores can co-exist by exploiting different niches. In the Nairobi National Park in Kenya there are nearly 100 large plant-eating mammals per square mile (40 per sq km). Some graze on selected grasses or even particular parts of a plant. Browsers of different sizes reach different parts of the vegetation, so while giraffes feed on high branches, eland feed on lower leaves and twigs, and the tiny dik-dik antelope eats the lowest growth. Every species occupies its own niche and avoids direct competition with other species, although their needs may overlap. This diagram shows how different species divide up the grasslands.

FIGHTING OFF HERBIVORES
The acacia trees that dot the typical savannah scene (right) can tolerate the dry conditions and occasional burning of the grasslands. Besides having sharp thorns, they can also defend themselves chemically against the onslaught of browsing herbivores such as giraffes. When the acacia leaves are being eaten, the tree actively diverts toxic chemicals to its leaves, forcing the herbivore to stop eating that particular tree and move to another.

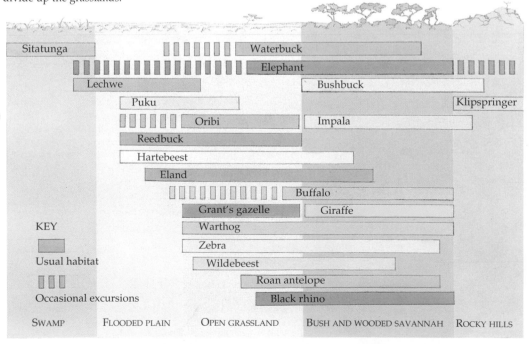

Sitatunga							Waterbuck				
Elephant											
	Lechwe			Bushbuck							
	Puku					Klipspringer					
		Oribi			Impala						
	Reedbuck										
	Hartebeest										
	Eland										
		Buffalo									
	Grant's gazelle	Giraffe									
	Warthog										
	Zebra										
	Wildebeest										
	Roan antelope										
	Black rhino										

KEY

Usual habitat

Occasional excursions

| SWAMP | FLOODED PLAIN | OPEN GRASSLAND | BUSH AND WOODED SAVANNAH | ROCKY HILLS |

COLONY'S COOLING TOWER
Termites, social insects rather like ants, construct these remarkable structures on open grasslands. A built-in ventilation system ensures that the queen termite is kept at a constant temperature, so that she can continue to lay eggs and maintain the numbers of termites in the colony, which can be several thousands. Termites use dead plant material as food, or grow fungus on it, which they then eat. Mongooses sometimes take over the mounds as homes. Termites are preyed upon by animals such as the aardvark.

MASS MIGRATION
On the Serengeti Plain in East Africa there are thought to be about 300,000 wildebeest, a species of antelope, in a 15,000-sq-mile (38,000-sq-km) region of grassland. Wildebeest are the most numerous primary consumers on the Serengeti, and they are the main source of food for lions and hyenas. At certain times of the year, vast herds of wildebeest migrate to seek water and fresher pastures and to breed. This mass exodus forces the predators to catch other prey, such as Grant's gazelle. These number around 100,000 in the Serengeti, feeding on grass and shrubs. They need far less water and therefore do not have to migrate.

SNAKE IN THE DRY GRASS
Reptiles are able to tolerate the conditions that exist on the grasslands during the dry season, and a wide range of snakes and lizards are found here. These include the slow-moving but highly venomous puff adder. Camouflage is very important in the grassland environment, especially during the dry season when the grass is short and sparse, providing little cover in which to hide. For this reason, many grassland species are dull brown-gray in color. Even the puff adder has to hide, as it is preyed upon by many of the savannah's large predatory birds, such as ground hornbills, eagles, and secretary birds.

Gray and brown coloring for camouflage in dry grass

Light markings to break up outline

Where river meets sea

IN THE ESTUARY, fresh water from rivers enters the sea, creating a rich and fertile ecosystem that is almost as productive as a coral reef (p. 46) or a tropical forest (p. 56). Most environments depend on plants to create the first energy source, but estuaries are also fed by a constant supply of mud, silt, the remains of plants, and other organic material, or detritus, brought down by the rivers, which mixes with material brought in by the tides. Even when this material muddies the water and prevents plants from photosynthesizing, the material itself provides a rich supply of food. This ensures that the few species that can tolerate the changing salinity (salt concentration) in the estuary achieve very large numbers.

FLATFISH
The flounder thrives in estuaries, where it feeds on the abundant worms, crustaceans, and mollusks such as cockles. The combination of salt and fresh water in the estuary poses a problem for many species, but the flounder can tolerate such a wide range of salinity that it is often found far upstream in the fresh water of rivers.

Jaws and tentacles

SLIMY PREDATOR
The ragworm has powerful jaws, as well as tentacles that allow it to feel its way through the muddy water in search of its prey of worms and even small fish. It also uses the vast supplies of detritus by making a sheet of slimy mucus with which it filters out the mud.

SUCCESSFUL MOLLUSKS
Some estuary species, such as the cockle (below), grow in vast numbers in estuaries, making the most of the abundant nutrients in the water and silt. Such productivity has led to the commercial gathering of these and other shellfish, and of crustaceans such as shrimps, creating a profitable industry. Cockles and other bivalve mollusks live in the silt on the estuary bed, sucking the rich mud up through an inhalent siphon and passing it through the gut.

PLENTIFUL TIDDLERS
Smelts are small fish that, like salmon, migrate upriver to lay their eggs. Such fish, which move from salt to fresh water in order to spawn, are described as anadramous. Some undergo physical changes while in the estuary in order to survive this change of habitat.
Smelts are found in very large numbers, and they form a food source for many species of fish, including salmon, cod, and halibut. Estuaries provide a rich and secure nursery for the growth of economically important fish worldwide.

ARMORED TUBES
The pipefish (right) is an occasional visitor to the estuary, where it feeds on crustaceans with its long tubular mouth. The thin pipelike body is kept rigid by a layer of bony armor under the skin.

SCENE FROM ABOVE
This satellite image shows the silty waters of the vast Ganges Delta in Bangladesh. The nutrients and silt form clumps that fall to the bottom, building up the rich muds at a rate of up to 0.08 in (2 mm) every year.

DINING ON SHELLFISH
Wading birds, such as these oystercatchers, feed on the plentiful supplies of mollusks, smashing them open on stones or using their sharp bills to pry the shells apart.

SPINY-BACKED FISH
There are many different species of stickleback. Some live in salt water, while others prefer fresh water. They all have protective plates rather than scales. Fresh-water species have fewer plates than those in the sea, and estuary species show an intermediate number, though it is not known why. The tiny three-spined stickleback (below) is found throughout the estuaries of the Northern Hemisphere.

BOTTOM FEEDER
The gray mullet is a truly euryhaline fish, meaning that it can survive in a wide range of salinities. It feeds on fine algae and detritus on the estuary bed. It takes in unfiltered mud and churns this in its thick-walled, muscular stomach to remove and digest any particles of food.

HUNTING IN THE GLOOM
The bass is one of the estuary's carnivores, feeding on other pelagic (mid-water) fish such as the smelt. In common with many other predators, it is capable of fast bursts of speed and has sharp teeth for grasping prey. Although primarily a marine fish, the bass is euryhaline and is perfectly at home in the brackish (slightly salty) estuary waters.

FIXING THE SILT
Cord grass, or *Spartina*, plays an important role in changing the estuarine landscape. Growing quickly in the shifting muds and silts of the estuary shallows, the grass holds the mud in position with its roots, allowing further silt to accumulate and gradually form mud flats, salt marshes, and even reclaimed land, as other plants manage to take hold.

Scaling the heights

THE MOUNTAIN ENVIRONMENT is a harsh one, and the higher the altitude, the harsher it becomes. The temperature falls by about 1°C for every 500 ft (150 m), the winds blow harder, and the atmosphere becomes thinner and less rich in oxygen. Thin soils, high winds, and low temperatures cause many plants to grow in a stunted form, giving rise to dwarf varieties that can survive mountain conditions. Most mountains are covered in snow for some of the time, and conditions can closely resemble those in semipolar, or tundra, regions. Several species of animals and plants adapted for life in the tundra were left behind when the melting ice sheets retreated northwards at the end of the last Ice Age. In the mountains, these species found conditions very similar to those of the tundra, and they were able to remain there, sometimes evolving in isolation from other populations. This is one of the reasons why mountain life varies so much from region to region. Most of the examples seen here are found in northern Europe.

Snow field to summit

14,000 ft (4,200 m)

Rocky scree

Alpine tundra

Alpine meadow

8,500 ft (2,600 m)

Coniferous forest

Deciduous woodland of the foothills

MOUNTAIN ZONES
These are the changing layers of vegetation that occur on the south side of a tall mountain in the Alps, a mountain range in Europe. Deciduous woodlands clothe the foothills, giving way to coniferous forest, which can tolerate the increasing cold. At 8,000 ft (2,600 m), the alpine meadow, with its characteristic miniature slow-growing plants, is the main vegetation. Between the meadow and the snow field at the very top lies the alpine tundra with rocky scree above it. Whether a mountain is in the tropics or in a temperate region, the increasing altitude creates distinct zones of very different natural habitats.

LICHENS AS INDICATOR SPECIES
Lichens are an association between an alga and a fungus. In many species the relationship probably started off as a parasitic one, but now each organism depends on the other for its effective survival. They are important plants on a mountain, as they represent the first stages of colonization of bare rock, opening up opportunities for other life to find a foothold. Lichens are one of the organisms that provide ecologists with an effective tool for measuring the effects of a human activity on the environment. They are extremely sensitive to air quality, and as such they can be used as indicators of air pollution. Few lichens grow in cities or industrial regions, but further away from the pollution the diversity of lichens increases, and the species found will change. Lichens that have a treelike form indicate good air quality.

Treelike form indicating clean air

Cladonia species

Cladonia coniocraea

Hypogymnia physodes

Leaflike form

Cladonia species

Foliose lichen

ACID SURVIVOR
Much of the soil on mountain and upland regions is badly drained and waterlogged. Levels of oxygen in the water are very low, and in such conditions very little decomposition of plant material takes place. As the dead plant matter accumulates it forms peat, and this makes the water acidic. There are a few plants that can thrive in these conditions, including sphagnum moss (below). This moss grows so thickly that it forms "blanket bogs," and these encourage the continued formation of peat. Where woodlands have become waterlogged, sphagnum moss has been known to build up and completely bury the trees.

Foliose lichen

Sphagnum moss

SKY FIGHTER
Fast and agile in the air, with a keen eye and rapid reflexes, the merlin is one of the top predators in the mountain food chain. It takes small birds, such as meadow pipits and snow buntings, in mid-air. In winter, as food resources dwindle, it extends its feeding range to include pastures, marshes, and coasts.

SUMMER BREEDER
The snow bunting, seen here in winter plumage, is a characteristic species of the tundra in both Eurasia and America. It migrates south for the hardest months of the winter.

LEFT BEHIND
The mountain hare is well adapted for cold conditions, with small ears to reduce heat loss and a white coat in winter for camouflage. Like some other tundra dwellers, the mountain hare remained on mountains when the ice retreated north at the end of the last Ice Age.

LATE DEVELOPERS
The northern form of the oak eggar moth is darker than its southern relative, enabling it to absorb the Sun's heat more rapidly. Its life cycle is also adapted to harsh conditions. The larvae hatch in late summer and soon hibernate until spring, when the caterpillars feed on fresh heather and other plants. They then spend a second winter as pupae and emerge as adults in their third year.

CHARACTERISTIC COVER
Heather covers much of the land below the scree zone in mountain areas of Europe. On Scottish moors, red grouse are encouraged by deliberate burning of the heather in a mosaic pattern, to provide green shoots on which they can feed, as well as sufficient cover for nesting.

Caterpillar of oak eggar moth

Bog myrtle

Heather

Fresh waters

THE FRESHWATER ENVIRONMENT is more variable than the sea. The chemical composition is often affected by the rock type over which the river flows or on which a lake has formed. Where there is a rich supply of nutrients, encouraging the growth of plants, there will be a large number and variety of animals, such as insect larvae, fish, and birds. Nutrient-rich water is described as "eutrophic," and this condition can be brought about by human activities – for example by the input of excessive amounts of nutrients from agricultural fertilizers (pp. 17 and 21) or other forms of pollution. Nonproductive waters are known as "oligotrophic," and they tend to be in highland areas, particularly over hard rocks that do not erode easily. Such water is often clear and rich in oxygen, but poor in aquatic life. The ecology of fresh water is therefore complicated by these different factors. Some organisms are able to live in fast-flowing rivers, while others need the still, murky waters of a lake.

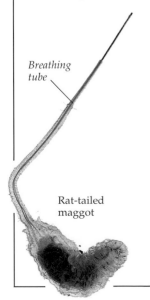

TAGGED FISH
Ecologists tag individual fish to determine the size of the population. This can be calculated using a formula based on the frequency with which the tagged fish are recaptured. By regularly weighing and measuring the tagged fish, ecologists can see how the condition of each one changes over time. Rates of growth are an indication of the prevailing ecological conditions. Tagging also helps in assessing the distances over which fish will travel.

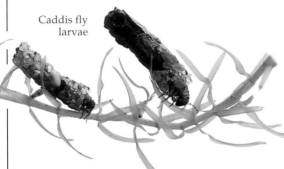

Caddis fly larvae

POSITIVE INDICATORS
In all rivers there is a profusion of small invertebrates under stones and among the plants. Many of these, such as the caddis fly larva, mayfly nymph, and bloodworm, are actually the larval form of flying insects. Their adult phase may be very short – only 24 hours in the case of some mayfly species, just long enough for the adults to breed and produce the next generation of insects. Some of these animals are particularly sensitive to pollution. Ecologists can therefore tell if part of a river is polluted simply by using a net to collect invertebrates over a given time period, and then counting the numbers of each species found. From this, an index of the biological diversity can be calculated. The effects of industries, sewage works, and other human activities can be monitored on a regular basis using this simple biological index. The presence of caddis fly larvae, mayfly nymphs, and water shrimps indicates clean water.

Mayfly nymphs

Gammarus water shrimp

WATER CROWFOOT
Like many plants found in streams and rivers, the water crowfoot is adapted to resist the pull of the current. It puts down strong roots in the riverbed, and its leaves have long thin stems, which bend in the flow of the water. The flowers of the water crowfoot emerge from the river surface and open in the air.

Breathing tube

Bloodworm

Rat-tailed maggot

NEGATIVE INDICATORS
If the netting of invertebrates in a stretch of river produces only such species as rat-tailed maggots, bloodworms, and tubifex worms, this tells the ecologist that the water is heavily polluted. Other forms of invertebrate life may not have survived either because their external gills have been clogged up by particles in the water or because they have been unable to tolerate a low level of oxygen in the water. The rat-tailed maggot (the larva of a fly) can survive these conditions because it takes in air from above the water surface, using a breathing tube rather like a snorkel. The tubifex worm needs little oxygen because it can use other elements to keep it alive.

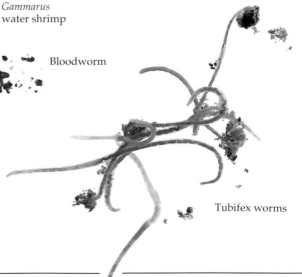

Tubifex worms

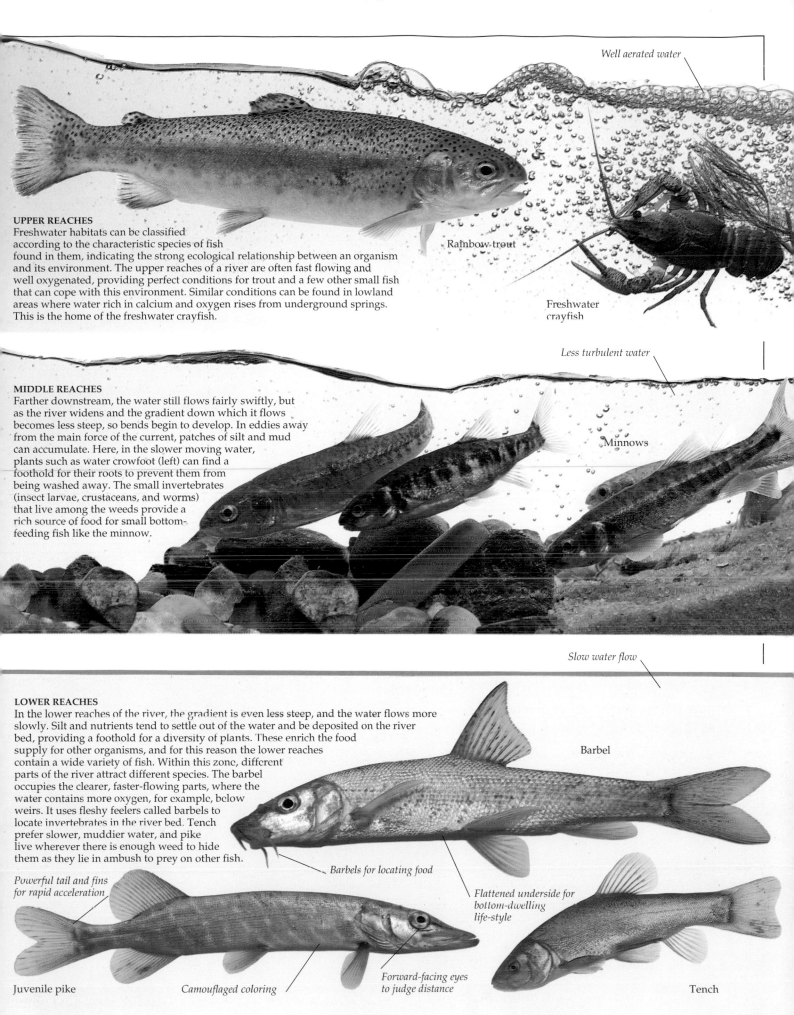

UPPER REACHES

Freshwater habitats can be classified
according to the characteristic species of fish
found in them, indicating the strong ecological relationship between an organism
and its environment. The upper reaches of a river are often fast flowing and
well oxygenated, providing perfect conditions for trout and a few other small fish
that can cope with this environment. Similar conditions can be found in lowland
areas where water rich in calcium and oxygen rises from underground springs.
This is the home of the freshwater crayfish.

Well aerated water

Rainbow trout

Freshwater
crayfish

MIDDLE REACHES

Farther downstream, the water still flows fairly swiftly, but
as the river widens and the gradient down which it flows
becomes less steep, so bends begin to develop. In eddies away
from the main force of the current, patches of silt and mud
can accumulate. Here, in the slower moving water,
plants such as water crowfoot (left) can find a
foothold for their roots to prevent them from
being washed away. The small invertebrates
(insect larvae, crustaceans, and worms)
that live among the weeds provide a
rich source of food for small bottom-
feeding fish like the minnow.

Less turbulent water

Minnows

LOWER REACHES

In the lower reaches of the river, the gradient is even less steep, and the water flows more
slowly. Silt and nutrients tend to settle out of the water and be deposited on the river
bed, providing a foothold for a diversity of plants. These enrich the food
supply for other organisms, and for this reason the lower reaches
contain a wide variety of fish. Within this zone, different
parts of the river attract different species. The barbel
occupies the clearer, faster-flowing parts, where the
water contains more oxygen, for example, below
weirs. It uses fleshy feelers called barbels to
locate invertebrates in the river bed. Tench
prefer slower, muddier water, and pike
live wherever there is enough weed to hide
them as they lie in ambush to prey on other fish.

Slow water flow

Barbel

Barbels for locating food

*Powerful tail and fins
for rapid acceleration*

*Flattened underside for
bottom-dwelling
life-style*

Juvenile pike

Camouflaged coloring

*Forward-facing eyes
to judge distance*

Tench

Incredible diversity

Tropical rain forests are continuously warm and moist, so fruit and seeds are available all year round. In these stable and relatively constant conditions, animal and plant life has been able to diversify more than anywhere else on Earth. Only coral reefs come close in the diversity of their species. In temperate ecosystems there are few species, but great numbers of each. In the tropical rain forest there are vast numbers of different species, but not so many individuals of each. In temperate regions, the main reservoir of nutrients is the soil. In the warm, moist conditions of the tropical forest, nutrients released into the soil are quickly taken up by the plants, leaving the soil thin and sandy. The trees themselves are the nutrient store, so if they are removed the ecosystem is disrupted.

HEAT-SEEKING STRIKER
Cook's tree boa lives in the canopy in the forests of northern South America. Like the forest monkeys, this snake relies upon its strong prehensile tail to travel through the trees. Taking a firm hold with its tail, it extends its body upward, wraps its fore end around a branch, and then draws the rest of its body after it. From a secure vantage point, it awaits its prey, such as the corollia bat (opposite), which it can spot using heat-sensitive pits on its lips. It then lunges out and catches its dinner in mid-air.

Heat-sensitive pit

UPSIDE DOWN
The three-toed sloth hangs by its claws from branches, moving slowly through the canopy and rarely descending to the forest floor. It is a major consumer of the leaves of one plant – the cecropia. It is partly camouflaged by green algae that grow in its damp fur, but it falls prey to jaguars and eagles.

Emergents

Canopy layer

Middle layer

Shrub layer
Ground layer

LAYERS OF THE FOREST
The canopy of the tropical forest forms a continuous platform of branches. Since this layer receives the full benefit of the sunlight, the fruits and flowers are to be found here, along with the animals that they attract. Plants that need less light live in the shadows below. At ground level there are the few plants that can flourish when a tall tree dies and lets the light through briefly.

LARGE-SCALE DESTRUCTION
Every year a region of tropical rain forest the size of Belgium is cut down or damaged, usually to open up the land to grazing or agriculture, but within about four years the soil becomes impoverished. Little can then be grown on it. Trees and nutrients are lost, and the unique diversity of the forest is also destroyed. Some of the disappearing plant and animal life could be economically important, and much has never even been described.

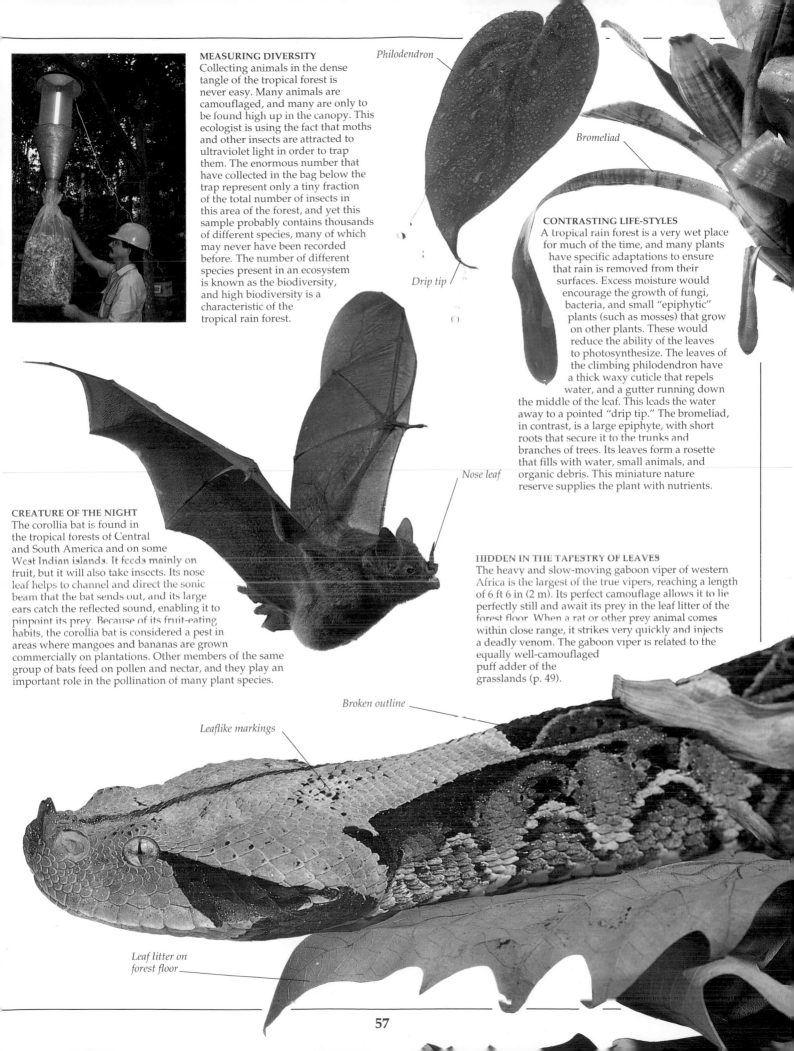

MEASURING DIVERSITY

Collecting animals in the dense tangle of the tropical forest is never easy. Many animals are camouflaged, and many are only to be found high up in the canopy. This ecologist is using the fact that moths and other insects are attracted to ultraviolet light in order to trap them. The enormous number that have collected in the bag below the trap represent only a tiny fraction of the total number of insects in this area of the forest, and yet this sample probably contains thousands of different species, many of which may never have been recorded before. The number of different species present in an ecosystem is known as the biodiversity, and high biodiversity is a characteristic of the tropical rain forest.

Philodendron

Bromeliad

Drip tip

CONTRASTING LIFE-STYLES

A tropical rain forest is a very wet place for much of the time, and many plants have specific adaptations to ensure that rain is removed from their surfaces. Excess moisture would encourage the growth of fungi, bacteria, and small "epiphytic" plants (such as mosses) that grow on other plants. These would reduce the ability of the leaves to photosynthesize. The leaves of the climbing philodendron have a thick waxy cuticle that repels water, and a gutter running down the middle of the leaf. This leads the water away to a pointed "drip tip." The bromeliad, in contrast, is a large epiphyte, with short roots that secure it to the trunks and branches of trees. Its leaves form a rosette that fills with water, small animals, and organic debris. This miniature nature reserve supplies the plant with nutrients.

Nose leaf

CREATURE OF THE NIGHT

The corollia bat is found in the tropical forests of Central and South America and on some West Indian islands. It feeds mainly on fruit, but it will also take insects. Its nose leaf helps to channel and direct the sonic beam that the bat sends out, and its large ears catch the reflected sound, enabling it to pinpoint its prey. Because of its fruit-eating habits, the corollia bat is considered a pest in areas where mangoes and bananas are grown commercially on plantations. Other members of the same group of bats feed on pollen and nectar, and they play an important role in the pollination of many plant species.

HIDDEN IN THE TAPESTRY OF LEAVES

The heavy and slow-moving gaboon viper of western Africa is the largest of the true vipers, reaching a length of 6 ft 6 in (2 m). Its perfect camouflage allows it to lie perfectly still and await its prey in the leaf litter of the forest floor. When a rat or other prey animal comes within close range, it strikes very quickly and injects a deadly venom. The gaboon viper is related to the equally well-camouflaged puff adder of the grasslands (p. 49).

Broken outline

Leaflike markings

Leaf litter on forest floor

Human ecology

ECOLOGICALLY, EARLY HUMAN BEINGS were much like any other species. They were a natural part of a food web, probably as primary consumers (pp. 10-11), being consumed in their turn by larger and more powerful secondary consumers. With the development of tools, the use of fire, and increasing communication skills, humans moved up the trophic pyramid to become hunters – secondary or even tertiary consumers – but their numbers were still limited by the energy available from the trophic level below them. Even with a wide repertoire of skills and tools, hunter-gatherers cannot exceed the carrying capacity (pp. 32-33) of the natural environment. The deliberate cultivation of crops changed everything, enabling human beings to increase the productivity of the land and escape the tyranny of the food chain. This single development makes humans ecologically different from all other species. It opened up the possibility of a tremendous population increase and has changed the face of the Earth itself.

DOMESTICATING WILD PLANTS
These different species of grass show some of the stages in the evolution of wild grass into modern wheat. The changes were produced by artificial selection, as people chose the seeds of those plants that had the largest seeds or other desired qualities. Wheat now provides an essential element in the human diet. Other crops were developed in other parts of the world, but all were members of the grass family. Agriculture fundamentally altered people's relationship with the environment, by creating a fairly predictable supply of food that could be stored and used on demand. Humans became less directly dependent on natural conditions, settled ways of life developed, civilizations grew up, agricultural techniques steadily improved, and the human population began to grow.

Spelt – a cross between emmer and wild goat grass

Wild emmer – ancestor of emmer

EARLY ENERGY SUBSIDY
The discovery of how to make fire, using simple tools like this African fire drill, opened the way for early humans to exploit new sources of energy in the environment. It enabled them to cook and eat previously unusable kinds of food.

HUNTING AND GATHERING
Throughout most of human history, human beings have been hunter-gatherers, with a way of life based on gathering wild plant materials, such as energy-rich seeds and fruit, and killing the occasional animal to supplement the diet. Some Australian Aboriginal peoples still live like this. Such a way of life requires an intimate knowledge of the natural environment, its particular characteristics and seasonal changes, and in this sense hunter-gatherers have certainly been in tune with their environment. It also makes settled communities impossible, since hunter-gatherers must always be on the move, roving large areas in search of new sources of food.

Emmer seeds

Emmer – main cereal in Greek and Roman times

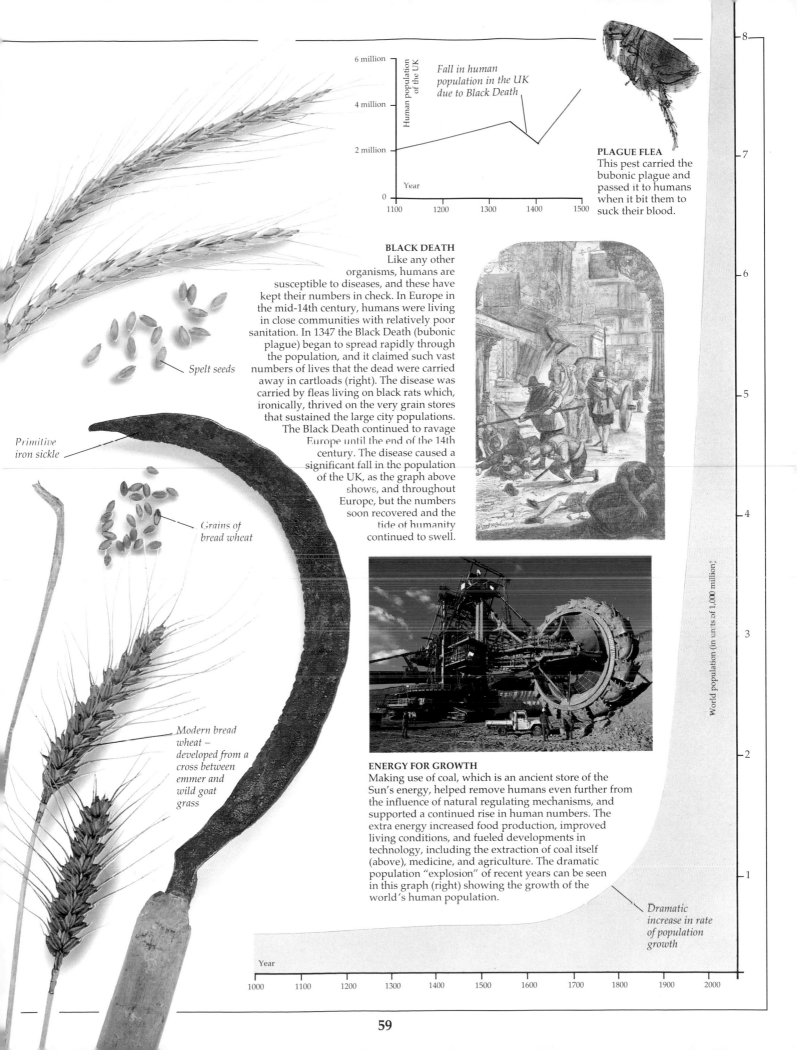

Fall in human population in the UK due to Black Death

Human population of the UK

6 million

4 million

2 million

0

Year

1100 1200 1300 1400 1500

PLAGUE FLEA
This pest carried the bubonic plague and passed it to humans when it bit them to suck their blood.

Spelt seeds

Primitive iron sickle

Grains of bread wheat

Modern bread wheat – developed from a cross between emmer and wild goat grass

BLACK DEATH
Like any other organisms, humans are susceptible to diseases, and these have kept their numbers in check. In Europe in the mid-14th century, humans were living in close communities with relatively poor sanitation. In 1347 the Black Death (bubonic plague) began to spread rapidly through the population, and it claimed such vast numbers of lives that the dead were carried away in cartloads (right). The disease was carried by fleas living on black rats which, ironically, thrived on the very grain stores that sustained the large city populations. The Black Death continued to ravage Europe until the end of the 14th century. The disease caused a significant fall in the population of the UK, as the graph above shows, and throughout Europe, but the numbers soon recovered and the tide of humanity continued to swell.

ENERGY FOR GROWTH
Making use of coal, which is an ancient store of the Sun's energy, helped remove humans even further from the influence of natural regulating mechanisms, and supported a continued rise in human numbers. The extra energy increased food production, improved living conditions, and fueled developments in technology, including the extraction of coal itself (above), medicine, and agriculture. The dramatic population "explosion" of recent years can be seen in this graph (right) showing the growth of the world's human population.

World population (in units of 1,000 million)

8
7
6
5
4
3
2
1

Dramatic increase in rate of population growth

Year

1000 1100 1200 1300 1400 1500 1600 1700 1800 1900 2000

Human impact

SINCE THE INDUSTRIAL REVOLUTION of the 18th and 19th centuries, human impact on the environment has been enormous. The burning of fossil fuels has polluted vast areas and significantly altered the atmosphere. Industrial technology has brought millions of people from rural areas into new towns and cities, and advances in mechanization have dramatically reduced the number of people needed to work the land. The use of fertilizers and pesticides has increased agricultural production and fed the growing human population, but these chemicals have had dire effects. The consequences of all these rapid changes could not be predicted. Now the science of ecology has made it possible to assess how human actions affect the environment and to look for ways to reduce and repair the damage that is being done.

TREATING THE SYMPTOMS
Cyclists in some cities already feel the need to protect themselves against atmospheric pollution from traffic. Technological solutions, such as face masks, may deal with the symptoms of an environmental problem, but the root causes of many of the problems, such as too many vehicles on the roads, are far more difficult to solve.

THE PRICE OF A SHORT-TERM VIEW
The increasing demand for food, and advances in technologies for locating, catching, and processing fish, have put enormous pressure on fish populations. Certain fisheries, such as the herring fishery in the North Sea and the anchovy fishery off the coast of Peru, have collapsed completely as a result of overfishing. Ecologists recognize the need to allow wild populations of animals, such as fish, to breed in sufficiently large numbers to ensure their continued existence. Sadly, the value of today's catch is often given priority over the need to conserve for tomorrow. This can result in disaster for the fish, and ultimately for the people who depend on them. It should be possible to achieve a balance by only taking sustainable yields (p. 63).

INTO THE ATMOSPHERE
A skyline of tall chimneys and cooling towers belching plumes of smoke and steam from industry, chemical plants, and power generators is now a common sight across the industrialized world. The environmental price of this technology is becoming all too obvious.

Cabbage leaf

Caterpillar of cabbage white butterfly

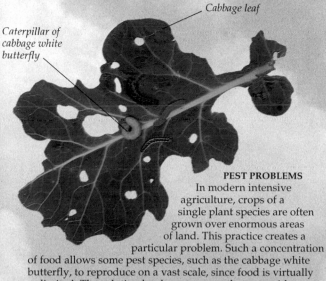

PEST PROBLEMS

In modern intensive agriculture, crops of a single plant species are often grown over enormous areas of land. This practice creates a particular problem. Such a concentration of food allows some pest species, such as the cabbage white butterfly, to reproduce on a vast scale, since food is virtually unlimited. The solution has been to spray the crop with pesticides. As a result, pest species build up a resistance to the pesticides, human food crops carry potentially harmful chemicals, and non-biodegradable chemicals gradually infiltrate the environment. Ecological studies have now led to the development of biological methods of control (p. 62-63).

BLOWING THE WHISTLE

After World War II, a new range of insecticides, including DDT, was hailed as a major weapon in the battle to eradicate pests and improve crop yields. No one considered the effect that these insecticides, which are not biodegradable, might have on the environment and on other living things. In 1962 Rachel Carson's book *Silent Spring* brought attention to the damage that these chemicals were doing. In her book, Carson presented evidence that insecticides were killing more than just pests. Secondary consumers were eating sprayed insects and were concentrating the pesticides in their own bodies. With each step up the trophic pyramid, the chemicals were becoming more concentrated, posing a particular danger to creatures at the top of a food chain, including human beings. Carson warned not only that there might come a time when bird song would no longer herald the spring, but that human beings are threatening their own existence.

WHAT A WASTE

Many complex manufactured chemicals, including plastics and some metals, cannot be broken down by decomposers. They remain in the environment, permanently locking away the natural resources that went to make them. More serious still is the dumping of poisonous chemicals, and there are many examples of hazardous waste leaking into the environment and harming both the ecosystem and people. Many people feel that until such materials can be disposed of safely, they should not be made.

Ecology today

Human beings are now the most influential creatures on the planet. Our activities, from energy use and mineral extraction to agriculture, industry, and urbanization, take place on such an enormous scale that the environment is being fundamentally altered. The composition of the atmosphere is changing. Water is being polluted at all stages in the hydrological cycle. Manufactured and often toxic chemicals are being used in pest control and in countless industrial processes. Populations of marine animals are being harpooned and netted despite the threat to their continued existence. Valuable resources are locked up in consumer goods and materials, and very little of this is recycled. The effects of human activities are endless and varied, but they all have one thing in common. Their long-term consequences cannot be predicted without a thorough understanding of the complex ways in which the biosphere works. Although ecology is not primarily about solving environmental problems, its goal is to deepen our understanding of the relationships between living things and between them and the physical world. Ecologists are already proposing ways of meeting human needs that are sympathetic to the environment, and drawing attention to the ecological implications of just about everything that humans do, but to solve the problems, people must want to use this knowledge.

THE GAIA THEORY OF LIFE ON EARTH
In 1979 James Lovelock, a British scientist but not an ecologist, proposed a theory of life, which he named after the Greek Earth goddess Gaia. The basis of his theory is that the Earth is a self-regulating organism that adjusts to changes in order to maintain suitable conditions for life (rather as warm-blooded animals regulate their body temperature). Lovelock's theory suggests that life on Earth will continue, no matter what humans do to it. The problem may be that the forms of life that survive may not include humans.

Euglandina snail

Partula snails

THE COMPLEXITIES OF BIOLOGICAL CONTROL
The giant African land snail, shown here life-size, was introduced on to islands in the South Pacific, primarily as a food source, but it was soon found to eat vast quantities of the natural vegetation and even some of the crops. To solve the problem, the much smaller predatory snail *Euglandina* was introduced, in the hope that it would keep the numbers down by eating the eggs of the giant snail. Unfortunately, *Euglandina* chose to prey on the even smaller native *Partula* snail, an innocent party in the affair. The *Partula* snails were completely wiped out on some islands. The situation is now being remedied by an international breeding program, and the *Partula* snail is being reintroduced to its previous habitats. A lack of ecological understanding contributed to the demise of *Partula*, which is now to be saved by ecology.

Giant African land snail

SAVED FROM EXTINCTION

The reintroduction of the buffalo to the Great Plains of the US, when this mighty animal was close to extinction, is a conservation success story. Recognizing the need for urgent action, concerned people set up a breeding program and eventually released a herd into a protected wild reserve. This apparently modern attempt to protect a species actually began in 1905. Today, international agreements are a vital part of wildlife conservation, but such agreements can only succeed if they are rooted in an understanding of ecological principles.

Water surface

Breathing tube

Mosquito larvae

Head

DISEASE CONTROL

Mosquitoes, which spread the deadly disease malaria, can be controlled with pesticides, but eventually the mosquito population becomes resistant. An ecological understanding of the mosquito's life cycle and its place in the food web have led to alternative solutions. By spraying a thin layer of oil on the water in which the larvae live, they are prevented from breathing through the tubes that they push up into the air, and they die. Biological methods include the introduction of a species of fish called *Gambusia*, which feeds on the mosquito larvae without having unwanted environmental side effects.

BURNING IVORY

The endangered African elephant has been given some protection by the creation of national parks, but the threat of illegal poaching persists. Poachers can get high prices for the elephants' tusks on the illegal ivory market. An international agreement to end the trade offers the elephant a chance of survival, and the President of Kenya has taken the dramatic step of burning his country's stock of confiscated ivory to show the ivory-carving industry that there will be no further supplies of their raw material. Through international agreements that implement the findings of scientific research, ecologists can now influence the survival of the organisms they study.

SUSTAINABLE YIELDS

Removing the youngest individuals from a population before they can reproduce themselves ultimately results in extermination, and this has led to the collapse of some fisheries. To prevent this, international laws now fix the minimum size of fish that can be taken, and fish in markets are measured to ensure that they meet legal requirements.

Mountain ash sapling

STARTING NEW GROWTH

The planting of a tree has taken on considerable symbolic value for the environmental movement, and for very good ecological reasons. Reforestation represents rebirth and a chance for a fresh start, but it is also a practical solution to many environmental problems. In many places the removal of trees has led to serious erosion (p. 23), and even desertification. Replacing the trees can help the land to recover. Trees also take up carbon dioxide and help reduce the atmospheric concentrations of this gas that have risen as a result of the burning of fossil fuels. Mixed deciduous woodlands also provide rich habitats for a wide diversity of species, unlike monoculture plantations of softwood trees.

Did you know?

AMASING FACTS

Sunlight is the source of energy for the Earth's oceans, atmosphere, land, and biosphere. This energy heats the Earth to temperatures far above the -454°F (-270°C) of deep space. It would take 1.7 billion power plants cranking out 100 million watts of power to equal the energy coming from the Sun—that's about one power plant for every three people on Earth.

Only one percent of the world's water is available for drinking. The oceans and seas contain 97 percent of the water as salt water, and another two percent is frozen in the polar ice caps. There is about as much water in the world today as there was thousands of years ago. And it is the same water—nature constantly recycles water through the water cycle. Water moves and changes forms, but it never disappears. So the water in your faucet could contain molecules once consumed by a thirsty dinosaur!

A glacier locks up water.

The portion of the Earth on which humans can comfortably live is small: Just 12 percent of the land area is populated by humans. When you factor in the oceans, that means humans occupy just four percent of the total surface area.

Dust and the way it moves across the globe has a profound impact on Earth's systems. Dust particles are created from a variety of natural sources, such as volcanic ash, pollen, bacteria, fungi, plant and animal fibers, and eroded bits of soil and rocks. Dust is lifted by the wind and transported vast distances as part of the Earth's recycling process. If dust clouds containing bits of soil and pollen had not been carried to the volcanic Hawaiian Islands from Asia, they would be completely barren and free of vegetation. Likewise, scientists have discovered that the rain forests of the Amazon depend on nutrients carried in dust clouds from Africa.

The word *smog* was coined in 1905 to describe the smoke and fog hanging over large cities. Scientists now divide smog into two categories: Photochemical (or brown-air) smog builds up in warm, dry, non-industrial cities such as Los Angeles and Mexico City, and is created mainly by automobiles and power plants. Sulfurous (or gray-air) smog is found in industrial cities with moist and cold climates, such as New York and London, and is created by factory smoke and sulfur oxides. Smog is a grave danger to the environment, since it kills or damages plants and can enter the water system when airborne pollutants fall to the ground in the form of acid rain.

Smog over a Singapore skyline

Ecologists concerned about the effect of habitat destruction on animal life have an important mascot: the flightless bird known as the dodo. This creature, with stubby wings and an ungainly body, was first spotted around 1600 on Mauritius, an island in the Indian Ocean. Less than 80 years later, the dodo was extinct. Some of the birds were eaten by the Dutch sailors who discovered them. But the main cause of their extinction was the destruction of the forest, which cut off the dodo's food supply, as well as the invasion of cats and rats, which arrived on the sailing ships and scavenged dodo nests.

Dodo

There is a good reason to hug trees. Trees not only release oxygen for us to breathe—they also help ensure the air we breathe is cleaner. A tree can trap and hold particulate pollutants such as dust, ash, pollen, and smoke in its leaves and bark, in addition to absorbing excess carbon dioxide.

Recycling is not a new idea. In the 18th century, people scavenged for bits of cloth to sell for use in paper production. These "rag-pickers" received about as much money for their bundles of cloth as someone recycling aluminum cans would get today. During the 1940s, recycling scrap metal and paper were a part of the war effort, but Americans saw little need to recycle after World War II. In the late 1960s, recycling was embraced by the environmental movement as a way to conserve energy and resources.

An oil spill is a discharge of oil into a body of water, such as when an oil pipeline ruptures or a tanker crashes. During the last decade, over a billion gallons (3.8 billion liters) of oil spilled worldwide. The amount of oil spilled doesn't always indicate how much damage the spill will do to the environment. The *Exxon Valdez* spill off the coast of Alaska in 1989, for example, was nowhere near the largest oil spill ever recorded, but it is widely considered to have done the most damage.

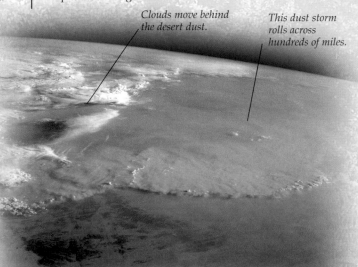

Clouds move behind the desert dust.

This dust storm rolls across hundreds of miles.

Duststorm over the Sahara Desert, Lybia and Algeria

QUESTIONS AND ANSWERS

Q How are Earth's species distributed?

A Biodiversity is not spread evenly across regions, or distributed evenly across biological groups. Over half of all described species are insects, for example. Scientists estimate that about 70 percent of the world's species occur in just 12 countries: Australia, Brazil, China, Colombia, Ecuador, India, Indonesia, Madagascar, Mexico, Peru (right), and Zaire. Tropical rain forests are believed to contain more than half the number of species on Earth.

A meandering river in the Pervuan rain forest

Q What is biodiversity? What does it include?

A Biodiversity (biological diversity) is a term to describe the immense variety and richness of life on this planet. It includes not only the many species that exist, but also the diversity of populations that make up a species, the genetic diversity among individual life forms, and the many different habitats and ecosystems around the globe.

Q How many species are living on Earth today?

A The basic unit of biodiversity is a species. No one knows how many species there are on Earth. The number of described species is around 1.75 million, but coming up with a more accurate figure is a difficult challenge. Areas of the Earth that were once thought to be mainly devoid of life, such as the bottom of the ocean, are now known to be teeming with organisms. Also, new species are being discovered in other habitats all the time. The black-headed sagui dwarf monkey (left), for example, was discovered in the Brazilian rain forest in 1996.

Q Why is conserving Earth's biodiversity a challenge?

A There is a growing concern that efforts are needed to conserve not just certain beloved species of animals (for example, pandas), but the diversity of life around the world, including many plants and animals that might never appear in the pages of a book or serve as the focus of an international conservation campaign (for example, slime mold).

Q What are the major risks to Earth's species?

A The major threat stems from human land use. As population growth explodes, more of Earth's surface is turned over to agriculture or foresting, putting habitats at risk. The introduction of species into new areas (either by accident or intention) is another major threat to species.

Q What is an endangered species?

A Endangered species—plants and animals in imminent danger of total extinction—are the focus of many international conservation programs. The World Conservation Union (ICUN) maintains a "Red List" of endangered species around the world. The species on the list are categorized as critically endangered, endangered, or vulnerable. In the United States, the U.S. Fish and Wildlife Service maintains the list of threatened and endangered species in America, state by state.

Q How many species are currently endangered?

A In 2004, a summary of data collected by the ICUN Red List showed that a total of 15,589 species face extinction. One in three amphibians, and almost half of all freshwater turtles are threatened, in addition to the one in eight birds and one in four mammals known to be at risk. The National Wildlife Federation estimates that 1,200 species are endangered in the U.S.

Q What is ozone? Is ozone good or bad for the environment?

A That depends on where it is in the environment. Ozone is a molecule made of three oxygen atoms (most oxygen molecules in the air have two oxygen atoms). It is made when sunlight acts on hydrocarbon pollutants in the air. On hot summer days in cities, ozone can build up near the ground, causing some people to experience shortness of breath or coughing. Ozone also causes damage to plants and animals. But while ground-level ozone is a curse, the ozone layer in the stratosphere is a blessing, providing a shelter against the sun's punishing ultraviolet rays.

Record Breakers

WORLD'S OLDEST TREE
The 4,768-year-old bristlecone pine known as Methuselah, in California's White Mountains, is the oldest tree in the world.

WORLD'S MOST MASSIVE LIVING THING
The General Sherman tree in California's Sequoia Park is 272 feet (83 m) tall. Its trunk is an enormous 35 feet (11 m) in diameter and 109 feet (33 m) in circumference at the base.

WORLD'S OLDEST PLANT
A creosote bush (a type of evergreen shrub) in California's Mojave Desert is estimated to have sprouted from a seed 12,000 years ago.

WORLD'S SMALLEST FLOWERING PLANT
The tiny green plants of the genus *Wolffia* could pass through the eye of a needle with ease. A "bouquet" of 5,000 plants could fit in a thimble.

WORLD'S LARGEST SEED
The gigantic Coco-de-mer (or double palm) seed of the Seychelles Island palm tree weighs a massive 66 pounds (30 kg).

WORLD'S LARGEST LEAF
The leaf of the raffia palm of tropical Africa can be up to 65 feet (20 m) long.

Zones of life

A BIOME IS A COMMUNITY of plants and animals living together in a certain kind of climate. Scientists have classified regions of the world into around 150 different biomes; the major biomes and some of the creatures that live there are featured on these pages. The importance of understanding biomes cannot be overestimated. Biomes have changed and moved many times during the history of life on Earth. Changes in the population of one organism in a biome can affect many populations in the same biome. More recently human activities (see pp. 60-61) have had a drastic impact on these communities. Conserving and preserving Earth's biomes should be a goal for the global community.

MOUNTAIN
Several distinct habitats exist from the base of the mountain to its peak. Most mountain animals are plant eaters. Small ones include voles, chipmunks, and chinchillas. Larger residents include the yak, mountain goat, ibex, chamois, and snow leopards, as well as scavenger birds like the condor (above).

Flat plains and rocky hills are found in scrublands.

BOREAL FOREST
Stretching in a vast belt through northern North America, Europe, and Asia, the boreal forests are covered in frost for most of the year. Animals found there include rams (above), caribou, elk, moose, wolves, and bears.

SCRUBLAND
In dry, temperate areas with mild winters and hot summers, scrubland biomes are found. Plant species found there include olive trees, cork oak, live oak, pine, and eucalyptus trees. Native animals include deer, small mammals, and birds (mostly ones that live near the ground).

Most scrubland plants grow low to the ground.

A cactus has tough skin to keep in moisture.

TUNDRA
The vast plains of Earth's frozen regions are called tundra. When the snow eventually melts in the short summers, the frozen ground is mainly bare except for streams running from glaciers, or pools of meltwater. As the ground begins to thaw, clouds of insects buzz through the skies and colorful flowers and tiny willow and birch trees grow. Geese and ducks migrate to the tundra in summer. Plant-eating mammals, such as reindeer, Arctic hares, and lemmings nibble the vegetation, while predatory wolves, foxes, and owls hunt the mammals.

DESERT
Nearly one third of the Earth's total land surface is covered in deserts. A desert is a dry place with less than 10 inches (25 cm) of rainfall per year. Desert animals include hares, camels, snakes, scorpions, lizards, and various birds of prey.

Scorpion

The tundra floor is in bloom.

SAVANNA

The grass-covered stretches of South America, Africa, and southern Asia are known as savannas. Large numbers of grazing animals live here. In the African savanna, for example, zebras, elephants, rhinoceroses, antelopes, and buffalo are nourished by the grasslands. They are hunted by large carnivores: lions, leopards, cheetahs, hyenas, and wild dogs.

Parrot

Herd of grazing zebras

Leaves change color as their chlorophyll slowly breaks down.

TROPICAL RAIN FOREST

Lush tropical rain forests have hot weather and plenty of rain. Altogether, more than 100,000 plant species live in rain forests, including mahogany, teak, rubber, and banana trees, as well as the plants that supply us with cocoa, coffee, ginger, and nutmeg. Monkeys and apes, big cats, bats, sloths, and many birds climb rain-forest trees. Amphibians, reptiles, and many insects live on the forest floor.

TEMPERATE FOREST

The temperate forest has plenty of rain and mild winters, but it is still cold enough to cause deciduous trees to shed their leaves in the winter. As dead leaves rot, their remaining nutrients sink into the rich soil. Trees in a temperate forest can live for hundreds of years, giving food and shelter to animals such as squirrels, jays, woodpeckers, mice, bats, and shrews. Deer also eat leaves and grasses, and wolves, lynxes, and elk prowl the woods.

TEMPERATE RAIN FOREST

Found on the western edges of North and South America as well as parts of Japan, New Zealand, and Australia, temperate rain forests have layers of tall, medium, and low vegetation, like tropical rain forests. But because there is a seasonal variation of temperature, there are less living things in the temperate forest. From mammals to amphibians to birds, most of the animals live on or near the ground, where there is food to eat and places to find shelter.

Snow still blankets the mountain peaks.

TEMPERATE GRASSLAND

The prairies of North America, the steppes of eastern Europe and Asia, the pampas of South America, the South African veld, and the downlands of Australia make up this biome. The Australian grasslands are home to kangaroos, while wild horses, antelopes, marmots, gerbils, and voles live in the European and Asian steppes. The American prairies have all but disappeared, due to the expansion of farming and the spread of suburbia.

Kangaroos usually rest in the heat of the day and are more active at night.

Kangaroos feed on grass and shrubs.

Green treelike plants dot the tundra.

Find out more

LEARNING ABOUT ECOLOGY helps us become better neighbors in the world. Here are some ways to find out more, and to make environmental action a part of your everyday life. Take a walk through a beautiful botanic garden to discover amazing examples of plant life. Visit a zoo or aquarium for up-close and unforgettable animal encounters. A national or state park is an excellent place to get an outdoor education—ranger-led walks and programs can be fun as well as informative. Universities and science centers may offer workshops or classes in environmental science, or you could join an ecology program to learn how you can make a difference in the world.

VISIT AN AQUARIUM
The beauty of the aquatic world is yours to discover on a visit to an aquarium. Like zoos, most aquariums participate in educational and conservation programs to help preserve and protect aquatic animals and habitats. Many places offer behind-the-scenes tours or classes so that you can find out more about what goes on behind the aquarium walls.

VOLUNTEER WITH AN ECOLOGY PROGRAM
You can do your part to protect the Earth's ecology by volunteering to help with an environmental awareness project. Many projects are organized around International Earth Day celebrations, but your efforts will be appreciated on any day. Whether you are planting trees or cleaning beaches, helping preserve the Earth and clean the environment is an important task, crucial to our future. Check the Internet for volunteering opportunities, or ask your science teacher if there is something you and your class can do.

USEFUL WEB SITES

www.ecology.com
Feature stories, news links, and a wealth of interesting information

nature.org
Home of The Nature Conservancy, dedicated to preserving Earth's diversity

www.oceanconservancy.org
The home page of the Ocean Conservancy, advocates for wild, healthy oceans

www.unep-wcmc.org
The latest news and updates from the United Nations Environmental Program's World Conservation Monitoring Program

BEHIND THE SCENES AT THE ZOO
A day at the zoo is a great way to encounter the world's wild animals. But behind the scenes, in the hidden zoo, staff professionals work with conservation groups, universities, governments, and other zoos to protect and preserve wildlife. Research teams study fields of science such as ecology, reproductive biology, and animal behavior, sharing their expertise to help protect at-risk animals. Contact a nearby zoo and ask about education programs linked to conservation.

VISIT A RECYCLING CENTER

Many communities now have places to recycle trash. Find out how the recycling process works by taking a tour of your community recycling center. Many recycling centers offer tours to coincide with national recycling awareness plans. Give your local center a call to schedule a tour.

Children helping with newspaper recycling

Hikers in the Glacier National Park, Montana

A WALK IN THE PARK

The U.S. National Park System, as well as state park systems and local departments of parks and recreation, run conservation programs to inform and educate the community about ecological issues. The programs often include lectures and guided nature walks, as well as volunteering opportunities. Contact the parks directly for more information.

GO TO THE HEAD OF THE CLASS

If you think you might be interested in becoming an ecologist, a great way to get started is by taking an environmental science class or workshop. Several universities and science centers offer classes as part of their community outreach programs.

VISIT A BOTANIC GARDEN

Explore the variety of plant life by visiting a botanic garden. Many feature gardens devoted to particular biomes, such as a desert cactus garden. Botanic gardens also house research centers dedicated to the conservation and preservation of plant species. Here, children stop and smell the roses in a garden in Washington, D.C.

Places to Visit

CHICAGO BOTANIC GARDEN, CHICAGO, IL
This award-winning garden features just under two million plants in its amazing collection.

BROOKLYN BOTANIC GARDENS, BROOKLYN, NY
A beautiful garden featuring a spectacular rose garden and an annual cherry-blossom festival

ATLANTA BOTANICAL GARDEN, ATLANTA, GA
An incredible 15 acres of outdoor gardens featuring a fantastic Children's Garden

FAIRCHILD TROPICAL GARDENS, CORAL GABLES, FL
One of the world's finest botanic gardens and a leader in plant research and conservation

HUNTINGTON LIBRARY, ART COLLECTIONS, AND BOTANICAL GARDENS, PASADENA, CA
This garden features approximately 15,000 kinds of plants from all over the world.

SAN DIEGO ZOO, SAN DIEGO, CA
The zoo is home to some of the world's rarest wildlife, and its conservation work helps prevent more animals from becoming endangered.

BROOKFIELD ZOO, BROOKFIELD, IL
Explore more than 200 wild acres at this zoo, or take a class or a behind-the-scenes tour.

CINCINNATI ZOO AND BOTANICAL GARDEN, CINCINNATI, OH
See 500 animals and 3,000 plant species at this zoo, picked as a family favorite.

PHOENIX ZOO, PHOENIX, AZ
This beautiful zoo is home to more than 1,200 animals and a range of education programs.

LOWRY PARK ZOO, TAMPA BAY, FL
More than 1,600 animals in lush habitats, plus rides, shows, and water-play areas make this a unique, family-friendly zoo.

SHEDD AQUARIUM, CHICAGO, IL
An awe-inspiring place to explore the world of amazing aquatic creatures

NATIONAL AQUARIUM, BALTIMORE, MD
Explore more than 560 species of animals.

Glossary

ATOLL A ring-shaped coral reef or string of coral islands in a circle, usually enclosing a shallow lagoon

AUTOTROPHIC Describes an organism that is capable of making food from inorganic substances. For example, green plants are autotrophic because they make food through photosynthesis.

BACTERIA Any of the many single-celled, microorganisms that break down the wastes and bodies of dead organisms, so their components can be used by other organisms. Bacteria may be helpful (in human digestion, for example) or harmful (causing illnesses such as strep throat).

BIODEGRADABLE Able to be broken down into basic materials, such as water, carbon dioxide, and nitrogen, by the actions of living things such as bacteria.

Siberian tiger, a carnivore

BIOMASS The amount of living matter in a given area, including all the plants, animals, and insects

BIOME A large ecological community characterized by similar vegetation and climate, and all the living organisms who make their homes there

BIOSPHERE The part of the Earth and its atmosphere capable of supporting life

BOREAL FOREST A forest ecosystem found within the higher latitudes of the northern hemisphere, with cold, dry air and coniferous trees

CARBOHYDRATE An organic compound that consists of carbon, hydrogen, and oxygen. Plants make and store carbohydrates as their chief source of energy.

CARBON CYCLE The complex series of reactions through which carbon cycles, or moves, through the biosphere

CARNIVORE An animal that primarily eats the flesh of other animals; a meat-eater

CHLOROPHYLL The green pigment in living plants that absorbs energy from sunlight, to provide the energy needed for photosynthesis

COMMUNITY In ecology, a group of interdependent organisms that inhabit the same region and interact with each other

CONIFEROUS FOREST A woodland composed of needle- or seed-leaf trees that do not lose their leaves in the winter. Firs, pines, and spruces are common coniferous trees.

CORAL REEF A complex tropical marine ecosystem built by colonies of tiny animals, called polyps, that secrete hard skeletons. As polyps die, they leave their skeletons behind and new animals grow there, building the reef.

DECAY The organic process of rotting; for example, through the action of fungi on wood

DECIDUOUS FOREST A woodland composed of trees that shed their leaves regularly at a certain time of year. In cool areas, deciduous trees shed their leaves during the fall.

DECOMPOSER An organisms that feeds on the dead tissues of plants and animals, speeding up the process of decomposition

DETRIVORE An organism that feeds on dead and decaying organic matter. What they leave behind is then consumed by decomposers.

Garden slug, a detrivore

DISTRIBUTION In ecology, a measure of where, and in what numbers, a particular species exists

ECHOLOCATION The sonar-like technique used by bats, dolphins, and other animals to navigate. The animal emits a high-pitched sound that reflects off an object and return to the ears (or other sensory receptors).

ECOLOGICAL NICHE The role a species plays in its environment, determined by how it uses available resources and how it affects other organisms

ECOLOGY The scientific study of the relationships between living organisms and their environment

ECOSYSTEM A community of plants, animals, and microorganisms that are linked by energy and nutrient cycles and that interact with each other and with the physical environment. An ecosystem can be a rotting log or an entire forest.

ENVIRONMENT An organism's surroundings; the complex set of external conditions that affect an organism or community, including natural resources and other organisms

EROSION The movement of soil or rock from one area to another by the action of the sea, running water, moving ice, rain, or wind

ESTUARY The mouth of a river where freshwater meets and mixes with salt water

EUTROPHICATION The process by which an excess of plant nutrients in a body of water can lead to the depletion of oxygen dissolved in the water, killing fish and other aquatic animals. Bodies of water undergo this process slowly as they age, but human interference can speed up the process.

EVOLUTION In biology, the process of change in the traits of organisms or populations over time

EXTINCTION The total disappearance of a species from the Earth

FOOD WEB A complex network of many interconnected food chains

FOSSIL FUELS Any of the fuels formed eons ago from decayed plants and animals. Oil, coal, and natural gas are fossil fuels.

FUNGUS A plantlike organism with no chlorophyll. Yeasts, molds, and mushrooms are all fungi.

GAIA THEORY The idea that Earth is self-regulating and adapts to change, like an organism, proposed by British scientist James Lovelock.

GROWTH RINGS The layers of wood laid down each growing season on a tree. These rings are visible when the tree is cut, and may be used to estimate the age of the tree. One dark and one light ring combined equals roughly one year of growth.

Fungal spores

HABITAT The place where a plant or animal species naturally lives and grows, or the characteristics of the soil, water, and biological community that allow the species to survive

HERBIVORE An animal that feeds mainly on plant matter

HUMUS Decomposed plant and animal matter that is part of the soil. Healthy soil contains about five percent humus.

INDIVIDUAL A single organism in a larger community

Armadillo, an insectivore

INSECTIVORE An animal that eats mainly insects or spiders. Insectivores tend to be small and most active at night.

MIGRATION the regular movement of a group of birds or other animals from one region to another for feeding or breeding purposes.

NITRATE a compound containing nitrogen and oxygen that can exist in water or air and can have harmful effects on the environment at high concentrations.

Snow geese migrating

NITROGEN A gaseous element found in the air and in all plant and animal tissues. Nitrogen is an essential component of proteins.

OLIGOTROPHIC Term applied to bodies of water that are nutrient-poor and contain little aquatic or plant life

OMNIVORE An animal that will eat both plants and meat

ORGANIC Relating to, or made from, living organisms

ORGANISM Any living thing that has, or can develop, the ability to act or function independently

Raccoon, an omnivore

PH SCALE A scale used to describe the acidity or alkalinity of soil or a solution. A pH value of 7 is regarded as neutral. Larger numbers are more alkaline and smaller ones are more acidic.

PHOTOSYNTHESIS The process by which plants convert light energy into chemical energy. Plants convert water, carbon dioxide, and sunlight into carbohydrates (sugars and starches) and oxygen. The oxygen in the Earth's atmosphere is produced by this process.

PIGMENT Any of various compounds found in plant and animal cells that create coloring

POPULATION A group of organisms of the same species that live in a given area

PRIMARY PRODUCER In an ecosystem, an organism that is able to make its own food. Algae and grass are examples of primary producers.

SAVANNA A biome characterized by trees and shrubs scattered among a cover of grasses

SCRUBLAND An uncultivated area covered with scrub vegetation (stunted trees or bushes)

SPECIES A group of organisms that share a unique set of characteristics and that are capable of interbreeding

SPORE A seedlike reproductive cell released by organisms such as fungi, moss, and ferns

Puffball fungi releasing spores

STOMATA Tiny pores on the surface of plant leaves that can open and close to take in or give out water vapor

SUBSOIL A general name for the layers of soil below the topsoil containing little, if any, organic matter

TEMPERATE Refers to a climate free from extreme temperatures

TOPSOIL The upper layer of soil that contains organic matter in the form of the decayed remains of vegetation, along with a variety of soil-dwelling organisms such as earthworms

TROPHIC PYRAMID A representation of the exchange of energy in a particular ecosystem (see pp. 10-11)

TROPICAL Relating to the frost-free regions near the Earth's equator

TUNDRA A cold biome dominated by lichens, moss, grass, and woody plants

WATER CYCLE The continuous circulation of water from the atmosphere to the Earth and back again, through condensation, precipitation, evaporation, and transpiration

Index

Acknowledgments

The publisher would like to thank:
Mike Quorm, Robin James and the staff of the Weymouth Sea Life Centre, Clifton Nurseries (Maida Vale), Michael Exeter of the National Rivers Authority (Thames Region), Sue Dewar, Frank Greenaway, Mark O'Shea, Peter Rodway, and Henry Schofield, for their advice and help with the provision of animals and plants for photography; Martin Stenning of the University of Sussex for his technical advice on scientific equipment; Sharon Jacobs for proofreading; Jane Burton, Peter Chadwick, Phil Crabb, Philip Gatward, Steve Gorton, Dave King, c. Laubscher, Andrew McRobb, Steve Schott, Karl Shone, clive Streeter, and Kim Taylor for additional photography.

Illustrations Stephen Bull, Richard Ward, and Dan Wright
Index Jane Parker

Publisher's Note No animal has been injured or in any way harmed during the preparation of this book.

Picture credits
t=top b=bottom c=center l=left r=right

Associated Press 63 cl.
Bettman 61tr.
Camera Press/William Vandivert 30tl.
Carnegie Institute of Washington 34tl. Bruce Coleman/David R. Austin 59br; /Jane Burton 27 cl, 32tr; /John Cancalosi 41bl; Alain Compost 25bcl /Peter Davey 49t, 49cl; /Francisco J. Erize 25cl; / Dr Inigo Everson 12tl; /M.P.L. Fogden 40c, 56cr; /Jeff Foott 19c, 29 tr, 63tl; /Oliver Langrand 53tl; /Gordon Langsbury 53c; / Luiz Claudio marigo 57tl; /M. Timothy O'Keefe 15tr; /Dr Norman Pye 21cr; /Hans Reinhard 17cl, 27tc, 41tr; /Leonard lee Rue 48cr; /Nancy Sefton 47cl; /Uwe Walz 51cl; /Bill Wood 47b; /G. Ziesler 16cl;

Ecoscene 56b; / J. Farmar 11cr; .Andrew D. R. Brown 23c.
Mary Evans Picture Library 15tl, 59 cr. Frank Greenaway 12tr, 36b, 37tl, 37cr, 37bl.
Greenpeace/Germain 63cr.
Hulton Deutsch 7tl.
Image Bank/Jules Zalon 13tc.
Sandy Lovelock 62tr.
National Academy of Sciences, Washington 32cl.
NHPA/Andy Callow 37tr; Scott Johnson 47cr.
Oxford Scientif Films 16tl, 19br, 38c, /Animals Animals 27bl, and Doug Wechsler 13tr; /Kathie Atkinson 27tr, 32tl, 38tl; /J.A. Cooke 31c; /Laurence Gould 24bc; /Alastair MacEwen 29cl; /John McCammon 29bl; /Richard Packwood 21bl; Michael W. Richards 32c; /Frithjof Skibbe 25cr; /Harold Taylor 9tr, 12br, 13bl; /David Thompson 31bl; /Ronald Toms 20bl, 54tl; /Kim Westerskov 60, 60c.
Planet Earth Pictures/Ken Lucas 41tl; /Steve

Nicholls 54cr; /James D. Watt 39ct.
Panos Pictures Trygve Bolstad 23b; /Heidi Bradner 61bl.
Royal Society /Dr Eric hulten 36tl.
Science Photo Library /John Burbridge 59tr; /Dr Gene Feldman, NASA GSFC 39tr; / Adam Hart-Davis 20cl; NASA 51tr; / Dr David Patterson 27tl.
University of Georgia, USA 9cr.
Zefa /P. Raba 40tl; /D. Baglin 58bl.

AP Wideworld: 65bl
Corbis: 64bc; Jonathan Blair 71cl; Dean Conger 64tr; Michael & Patricia Fogden71cr; D. Robert & Lorri Franz 71tl; Craig Hammell 68cl; Catherine Karnow 69br; Steve Kaufman 69tc; Layne Kennedy 65tr; Charles Mauzy 68-69bc; Gabe Palmer 68cr; Tom Stewart 69tl; Keren Su 70bl; LWA-Dann Tardif 69bl

Jacket images: *Front:* Corbis: Lester Lefkowitz (b).

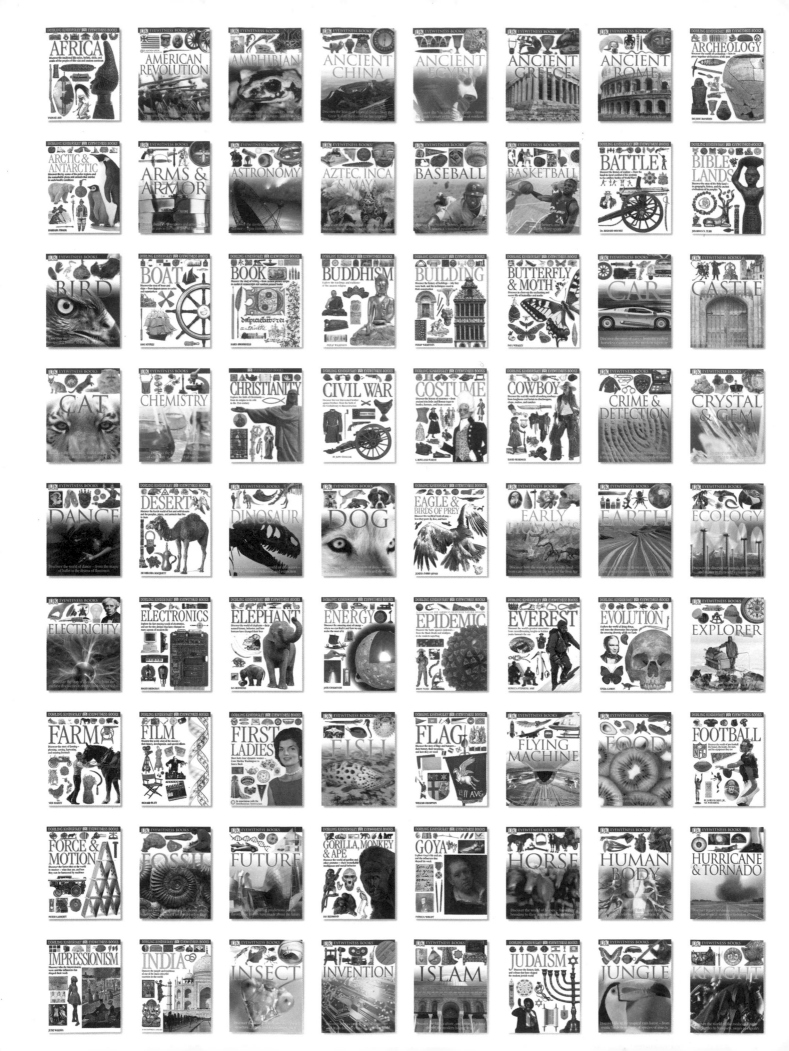